GOD WANTS
HIS KIDS BACK
Schools of Thought to Reach a Lost Generation

D1472502

"

God Wants His Kids Back expresses Nate's passion, creativity and perseverance in reaching out to a lost generation in our schools. His challenge is both intentional and practical, seeking to mobilize the Church, and joins God where he is already working.

Mike DeVito
Southwest Regional Coordinator
National Network of Youth Ministries

My heart breaks for this next generation. They are being raised fatherless and the pain in their stories is crushing them. They need hope and solid role models who will love them through their pain. In Dr. Landis' exceptional book, *God Wants His Kids Back*, you will gain the heartbeat and "how to's" for engaging youth relationally with the love, grace and hope of the Gospel.

Dr. Larry Acosta
Founder/CEO
Urban Youth Workers Institute

In *God Wants His Kids Back: Schools of Thought to Reach a Lost Generation,* my friend Nate Landis unpacks his burning passion to reach this next generation right where they live. He understands that the biggest mission field in the United States is the middle school and high school campus. In this highly inspirational book Nate gives a clarion call for each of us to do what it takes to reach these precious teenagers before it's too late. But this book is far more than inspirational. Nate delivers powerful and practical ways for you to join in the movement to reach this lost generation with true and lasting hope! Let's join Nate in this quest to give every teen everywhere every last chance to put their faith in Jesus!

Greg Stier
Founder and CEO
Dare 2 Share Ministries

Dr. Landis is a friend and a partner in ministry who desires to see God's kingdom revealed in our most diverse communities: our public schools. This book is full of useful tools that you can implement to make a difference in your local public school and, as a result, in God's kingdom.

Pete Contreras
Lead Pastor
New Vision Christian Fellowship

God Wants His Kids Back is a must-read for anyone passionate about serving youth and empowering them to be a light for Christ on their campuses. Dr. Nate Landis has been used powerfully by God to transform lives, schools, and communities for Christ.

Colin Sinclair
Southern California Regional Director
Fellowship of Christian Athletes

In John 17:21 Jesus prays, "I pray that they will all be one, just as you and I are one—as you are in me, Father, and I am in you. And may they be in us so that the world will believe you sent me." In sharing the gospel to inner-city San Diego teens the last 15 years through Young Life, the Lord has made it clear to me that we will need others. He has also made it clear that he has sent Dr. Nate Landis to spearhead the prayer of his heart in Urban San Diego. I thank God for the gift Dr. Nate and UYC are to San Diego County and this generation across the nation. The gift of unity and the good news of Jesus. Reading this book is reading the cry of God's heart and equipping oneself for action in reaching the next generation.

Jeremy Robinson
Area Director
Young Life (Inner-City San Diego)

GOD WANTS
HIS KIDS BACK
Schools of Thought to Reach a Lost Generation

DR. NATE LANDIS

GOD WANTS HIS KIDS BACK
SCHOOLS OF THOUGHT TO REACH A LOST GENERATION
by Dr. Nate Landis

Back cover: Content derived, in part, on research compiled by the Pinetops Foundation in a report titled *The Great Opportunity* (greatopportunity.org). Used by permission.

Unless Otherwise indicated, all Scripture quotations are from the Holy Bible, English Standard Version, copyright © 2001, 2007, 2011, 2016 by Crossway Bibles, a division of Good News Publishers. Used by permission. All rights reserved.

Scripture quotations marked (NLT) are taken from the Holy Bible, New Living Translation, copyright ©1996, 2004, 2007, 2013, 2015 by Tyndale House Foundation. Used by permission of Tyndale House Publishers, Inc., Carol Stream, Illinois 60188. All rights reserved.

New American Standard Bible. Copyright © 1960, 1962, 1963, 1968, 1971, 1972, 1973, 1975, 1977, 1995 by The Lockman Foundation, La Habra, Calif. All rights reserved.

Scripture taken from the Holy Bible: International Standard Version®. Copyright © 1996-forever by The ISV Foundation. ALL RIGHTS RESERVED INTERNATIONALLY. Used by permission.

Publication Design & Management:

LAMP POST *publishers*

lamppostpublishers.com

Published by:

URBAN YOUTH COLLABORATIVE
P.O. Box 124708 • San Diego • CA • 92112
www.uyc.org || www.natelandis.org

Trade Paperback: ISBN-13 # 978-1-7328354-0-5
ebook: ISBN-13 # 978-1-7328354-1-2

Dedication

I would like to dedicate this book to my late mother, Dr. Jean Myer Landis. As an urban educator and professor in Philadelphia, she taught me about Jesus' love for children who dare to dream big dreams despite facing longer odds in life. A passionate champion of Jesus, education, and justice, she shaped my life calling in ways I am only now beginning to understand. I love you and miss you, mom!

ACKNOWLEDGEMENTS

The kingdom work described in this book would not be possible without the tireless and dedicated efforts of the Urban Youth Collaborative (UYC) staff, student leaders, financial investors, church partners, teachers, administrators, coaches, parents, parachurch allies, and community organizations that believe in the limitless value of young people. An inspiring God-sized vision of a new city and a new version of youth ministry is too big to accomplish alone. We need the power of God and we need each other. Thank you for your friendship, sacrifice, and commitment to follow Jesus with me!

CONTENTS

PREFACE

On November 18, 2016, I stood up to speak in front of several thousand professional youth workers at the Youth Specialties' *National Youth Workers Convention* in Cincinnati. This annual event provides valuable training, networking, and renewal for many interdenominational youth ministers and pastors from across the country. That year, the conference coordinators invited me, along with several other campus ministry practitioners, to speak as part of their focus on churches engaging schools. Right before I got up on stage to talk, the hosts spontaneously polled the audience to find out how they are currently working with schools. They had technology available that allowed instant phone surveys to be calculated, so the results posted immediately on the large screen for all to see. The short questionnaire had some low hanging fruit on it, such as, "I'm praying for schools," "We are supporting parents," and "We are involved in campus clubs," to name a few. Despite those somewhat easy-to-claim options —nobody asked how often, deep, lasting, or productive the connections were – 47% of attendees selected the most popular response category which was: "Currently not doing any-thing at all." This was the most accurate way roughly half of this group of our nation's full-time youth pastors describe their congre-gation's present level of engagement with public schools in their community. While not totally surprising, that figure saddens me and motivates me to write this book. Almost half of this national sample of professional youth workers — and the broad swath of America's Christian churches they represent — spent zero time at the place where kids live the most: public school campuses. That's like a bunch of professional fishermen confessing that they spend no actual time out in the water.

The often misunderstood "separation of church and state" keeps many pastors and school administrators thinking they have no business ever crossing paths. There are legitimate challenges and understandable — yet surmountable — reasons why churches often overlook this vital locale for holistic youth ministry. I explore many of these factors in the pages that follow. I also touch on missteps some well-meaning churches and adminis-trators may take that cause unneeded apprehension towards one another. At the end of the day, schools and churches — along with the principals and pastors who lead them — are better off learning to dance together.

As we begin the conversation, let's take heart in Jesus' statement to his disciples. "Follow me," he says, "and I will make you fishers of people" (Matthew 4:19 ISV). Jesus promises to do on-the-job training for those willing to answer the call and follow him into the unknown — and at times uncharted — waters of public school min-istry. If we are not there yet, he can *make us* into leaders who dare to step out in faith and effectively go where the fish are. I pray this book equips, challenges, encourages, inspires, and moves you to do just that. I am here to tell you that fish usually travel in schools.

Fishers of men and women need to go where the fish are. If kids matter to Jesus, then they have to matter to his followers too. God is moving in our nation's public schools. Let's join him where he is already at work!

GOD WANTS
HIS KIDS BACK

Schools of Thought to Reach a Lost Generation

one

FISH TRAVEL IN SCHOOLS

The greatest day of my life was April 19, 2008. Early that morning, I became a dad for the first time. After my wife endured twenty-four hours of labor, Russell Anthony Landis came into the world weighing in at eight pounds, nine ounces. A sense of pure wonder filled the delivery room as I held him in my arms and looked deep into his clear blue eyes. He stared attentively back at me during our sacred encounter which changed me forever. I could see my face reflected in him, and he could see his face mirrored in mine. I thought to myself, "What a good-looking kid; he looks a lot like his dad!" No, I'm kidding. My first thoughts as a father centered on the fact that I was holding a little miracle in my arms. I donated some DNA to the project, but this was much bigger than me. I did not string his organs together inside his mother's womb. I did not tune his eyes to match the frequency of light on our planet. Nor did I place a hunger for eternity and transcendence firmly inside his soul. God did all those things, not me. In that breathtaking moment, I found myself the steward of another human life. What an awesome, scary, and humbling responsibility! A sense of selfless love for Russell instantly washed over me. For the first time ever, I personally felt a fraction of the love God must feel for every human being on planet Earth. Almost spontaneously, I began making commitments to my son. I promised to provide for him. I wanted to protect him. I vowed to do everything in my power to give him life to the fullest.

Then, without warning, two nurses hurried into the hospital room and fastened an electronic ankle bracelet onto my son's ankle. "Mr. Landis," they said, "do not take a wrong turn while holding your son in our hospital because we are monitoring his every move electronically." They continued, "If you go down the wrong hallway with Russell in your arms the entire hospital facility will immediately go into lockdown." I thought to myself, "Great, my kid is only two hours old and he's already on parole. I have already failed as a father." So I had to ask them why they put a baby LoJack on my son. One of the nurses explained that one out of every two thousand babies born in California get stolen from hospitals at birth.[1] Now, I have read different statistics about this. One source reports that baby abductions in hospitals are so rare that only one hundred seventeen recorded cases have taken place in the US since 1983.[2] But the point is the same. Despite the long odds, California hospitals detected a real threat and – because they value the life of every infant born under their care – now take definitive action to make sure that no baby gets lost on their shift. Loosing just one kid is completely unacceptable to California's hospitals.

As Jesus describes his heavenly Father in the New Testament, he speaks of an equally low acceptable casualty rate when it comes to children under his care. I believe the list of kids God cares about extends to every child on the planet. By the way, during the last minute spent reading this page, two hundred fifty new babies were added to the list of beloved young people on planet earth.[3] Despite the ever-growing number, God's love stretches infinitely to behold each of them. In Matthew 18:10-14, Jesus tells the parable of the lost sheep and makes it clear that his heavenly father is not willing to lose any sheep (which represent people) under his watch. He tells us the story this way:

> What do you think? If a man has a hundred sheep, and one of them has gone astray, does he not leave the ninety-nine on the mountains and go in search of the one that went astray? As if he finds it, truly, I say to you, he rejoices over it more that over the ninety-nine that never went astray. So it is not the will of my Father who is in heaven that one of these little ones should perish.

According to Jesus, then, God's acceptable casualty rate for kids in America (and globally) is zero. In my home city of San Diego – and I bet yours too – the math looks different than what Jesus lays out in this parable. Far more students are lost than just one. In fact, where I live, only 10% of public middle and high school students have a regular or meaningful relationship with a local church.[4] If hospitals are motivated to take definitive action with a much lower rate of child abductions taking place, how much more should God's people be motivated to act when the vast majority of young people in our cities are being lost spiritually? Let that question sink in. A careful reading of Jesus' words means that, as church leaders, we have to ask how willing we are to leave the 10% of kids in the youth group to lovingly go search for the 90% in our public school system. By taking no action, we settle for a higher youth casualty rate than either California's hospitals or Jesus are willing to accept.

The focus on public schools for which I advocate does not mean that we neglect or ignore the ten (percent of) kids who have already been found by Jesus. It simply means we make going after lost young people a priority like Jesus does. The ten found kids are already enjoying life to the fullest with the shepherd in the sheepfold. They are protected and experiencing all the goodness the shepherd wants for them. But there is still plenty of room in the sheep pen, and those outside – apart from Jesus – remain in very real danger. "The thief comes only to steal and kill and destroy," Jesus claims. "I came that they may have life and have it abundantly."[5] In Luke 19:10, Jesus goes on to describe his God-given mission by saying, "For the Son of Man came to seek and to save the lost." That is why Christ called his followers to join him: so we can go after lost people together. If our daily mission and passion differs from our master's self-described behaviors, can we accurately claim to be his followers? As Jesus himself says, "Not everyone who says to me 'Lord, Lord' will enter the kingdom of heaven, but the one who does the will of my father who is in heaven."[6] A disciple is a descriptive word for people who actively do what their master does. As people of faith and congregations in the US, are we willing to join Jesus in the God-given mission that he recruited his followers to complete? We are called to go into all the world and make disciples of all nations.[7] In America's public schools, the nations have come to us. The question for local churches now is not whether we dare to cross an ocean to bring the good news to others. We must simply muster the courage to cross the street.[8]

God the Father Has a Broken Heart

I grew up in the Mennonite tradition, a rich heritage that emphasizes the themes of non-violence, reconciliation, simplicity, communal living, and peace-making expressed through the teachings of Jesus, sections of the epistles, and formulations by Anabaptist theologians. Many of these worthwhile ideals still shape my life and ministry today. I am, for example, still registered as a conscientious objector to war of all types. But I have to tell you, if someone snuck into the hospital and stole my kid out from under my nose on the greatest day of my life, I would stop at nothing to get him back. I would go find some of my Baptist and Presbyterian friends who have no problem going to war – and who really know how to hurt – and we would go get my kid back at all costs. This same passion of the heavenly Father drove God to send Jesus to earth. He will not rest until the kids he loves are back safely in his arms.

Let me illustrate the father's love in a very practical way. May we do a little thought experiment together? Every summer, our ministry takes a hundred and fifty kids to camp at UCLA through our partnership with the Fellowship of Christian Athletes (FCA). Students from the inner-city get to experience life at a Division 1 university. They sleep in the dorms, eat in the cafeteria, play a sport of their choice all day, and then enjoy worship while hearing about Jesus in Pauley Pavilion – where the Bruins play basketball – every night. It is one of the best camps I have ever witnessed. This exhilarating week benefits students athletically, academically, and spiritually. God transforms the lives of many high school students through this experience each summer. For some, it is the first major trip they take outside of their own urban neighborhood and the first college campus they set foot on.

Imagine with me, though, if I take a hundred students – just to make the math a little easier – in several charter buses with me to camp. No matter how excited teenagers and parents are to be away at the beginning of a week of camp (years ago I once had a parent ask, "Can I pay you to keep my son for two weeks instead of one?"), everyone looks forward to the reunion in the parking lot when we return. If I leave with a hundred kids at the beginning of the week, how many students do parents expect me to bring back when I return? Rough estimates are fine. The interesting thing is, I have to come back with a hundred students every time...and they have to be the exact *same* kids too – funny how that works! Now let's take our thought experiment one step farther. What if I left with a hundred kids, came back, and got off the bus with only ten kids? Those figures match the estimated statistics for youth having a regular church connection in my home city. What would happen to me as a pastor? In some neighborhoods I would get sued, in some zip codes they would make sure I got fired, and then some parents would skip all the legal stuff and straight up jump me. Why? Because I lost *their* kid on *my* shift. If fallen, flawed earthly parents will not tolerate a 90% casualty rate for their own children, what makes us think our perfect heavenly father is pleased with similar numbers of kids going to school but never making it to church or Jesus?

What I would not be able to say to earthly parents after losing their kid is, "The students who made it back safely had a great time at camp." This misses the problem that so many are lost. Yet I often hear youth pastors and church leaders making similar statements when evaluating the health of their own church youth ministries. Statements like, "Most of the parents are feeling good about the youth group," or "the kids that are coming are having a great time," may not indicate that a proper measure of success has taken place, at least not the way Jesus defines it. Just because the majority of parents and the senior pastor are happy with the youth ministry does not necessarily mean that the kingdom of God is being advanced into the next generation or that new people are being reached and raised up as disciples. The higher standard and the larger question becomes, "Are we joining with Jesus to seek and to save the lost?" *As I asked earlier, if we do not do what our master is dedicated to, is it accurate to call ourselves disciples?* Since that is what Jesus came to do, we cannot claim to be his followers unless we dare to do the same. This is *our* shift, church. These are *his* lost kids in our cities, communities, schools, and neighborhoods. He wants them back. When we stand face to face with God the Father, he is going to ask us what we did with his kids on our shift.

It's been said that Christianity is only one generation away from extinction on every continent. Just like relay runners in an Olympic race, each generation must successfully pass the baton of faith they received during their leg. In our nation, we witness the baton hitting the ground with an echo whenever parents, churches, and others fail to effectively pass on the gospel they themselves received.

Researchers have documented the marked decline in church attendance and adherence to basic Christian doctrines from generation to generation in the US. From the Baby Boomers, to Generation X, to Millennials, to Generation Z, interest in spirituality, social justice, and diversity have steadily increased along with significant disinterest in classic Christianity. Distrust of institutionalized religion has also risen sharply. Josh McDowell's book *Last Christian Generation* and George Barna's research go so far as to make dire predictions about the percentage of Americans who possess a "biblical worldview." Should current trends of unbelief and doubt continue on the same trajectory for Generation Z – as they have for the group's parents and grandparents – current middle school and high school students will grow up in an increasingly secular – and largely post-Christian – society.[9] Suffice it to say that we must find a way to engage the coming generation of young people or else Christianity is headed for an accelerated decline in the

United States. I am far more concerned with the spiritual well-being of young people – now and forever – than with preserving some form of "Christendom" in America. Although the twilight of Christianity in the US would also mean the continued erosion of the many positive moral principles and values that accompany its true expressions. Therefore, we have lots of good reasons – both short term and long term – to continue pointing young people to Jesus.

When Christians withdrawal from public education and exclusively into the realms of private and home school environments, we may succeed at protecting children from some negative peer pressure and the detrimental content of certain public school curriculum materials. Nonetheless, if all the salt and light pulls out of the public school system, should we be surprised if we notice increased decay and darkness? Despite high distrust of institutional religion from Millennials and Generation Z, our ministry is witnessing a strong hunger for Jesus in public school students all over San Diego and in Mexico. We believe that the power of love and the security of truth – when fully experienced and properly grasped – has not gone out of style. Thanks to the life-giving properties they possess, *salt* and *light* will never become irrelevant when a generation actually *tastes* and *sees* that God is good!

God's Call in Front of a Public High School

My life changed forever one afternoon in 2006 as my Nissan Xterra sat at a red light beside a McDonalds and across the street from San Diego High School. Three thousand students go to school there and the majority do not have a regular or meaningful relationship with a local church. The congregation where I served as youth pastor sat just eight blocks away. Several years before, I approached the football coach and asked if he would be open to having a team chaplain. I explained that we could do pre-game meals and an optional motivational pep-talk before kick-off. As a local pastor and "life coach," I would make myself available to students for any life challenges that come up on and off the field. He responded by saying, "Sir, we were 1-9 last year. Prayer couldn't hurt!" That year he had eighteen academically ineligible players on the team who could not keep a 2.0 grade point average. I like to joke that it takes discipline to keep your grades that low. You need an accountability partner making sure you are not turning assignments in, not going to class, and being rude to your teacher.

On this particular afternoon, I was getting ready to pick up football players for the optional pre-game meal and chapel service that we put on for them at a nearby church. Suddenly, before I could do anything, the bell rang. A sea of faces from every tongue, tribe, and nation came pouring out into the intersection. I could not drive or I would have literally run some of them over. That's always a bad way to start a campus ministry – with injuries and hospital visits. So I had to just sit there in my car watching all these faces go by. The first thought I had at that moment brought great clarity to me. It went something like this, "These kids are never going to accidentally stumble into the well-endowed Presbyterian church castle I work at down the street," I confessed to myself. *If I build it, they will not come to me.* I am glad Jesus did not wait for us to stumble into our home in heaven on our own either. "And the word became flesh," the scriptures tell us, "and dwelt among us."[10] As Christ followers, we need to go to students, learn their language and culture, and meet them on their own turf. My second thought hurt to admit but flowed from the first observation. "If I bring any more of these urban kids into the youth group, there will be great debate inside the church about whether they should be there."

I had delivered on my promise to grow the youth ministry, but some parents privately questioned why I had to do it with *those* kids from surrounding public schools.

At that moment, I heard a still, small, inaudible but unmistakable voice that did not come from me. It asked, "Who *will* go for us? Who *will* reach these kids?" Immediately I started to cry, raised my hand in my heart, and whispered, "Here I am LORD, send me." That night after the football chapel and game concluded, I went home to my wife. We were eighteen months married at the time, had a mortgage, and live in the expensive land of Southern California. Presbyterians do buildings and budgets pretty well, so with a master's degree in Divinity, I had one of the few career path youth ministry jobs in the city with a solid salary, medical benefits, and a little retirement plan each month. "I've got a great idea," I told my wife. "I'm going to quit my job and go after the kids that not enough people are reaching." I didn't know what she would say, but without hesitating, she said, "I think that sounds fantastic sweetheart!" "Thank you, God," I thought to myself. No Christian small group would have given her flack for saying, "Let's pray more," or "Are you sure you heard?" She could have even found support for saying, "You're hearing voices in your car? Let's make an appointment with a good Christian shrink and I'll support you through the process sweetheart." But instead she was willing to risk it all and step out in faith because she could tell that God was up to something.

Fishers of Men and Women

When Jesus called Peter to leave everything and follow him, he said, "Follow me, and I will make you fishers of men (and women)."[11] I find this comforting because it says that Jesus is willing to do on-the-job training. He will *make* us into fishers of men and women if we are not yet already there. We just have to be willing to leave behind what we think our lives are supposed to be about and what we think we are good at. Then we *let* Jesus make us into what he had in mind when he created us. One important step in following Jesus and becoming a fisher of men and women is to realize that fish usually travel in *schools*.[12] (*Rimshot!* Thanks, I'll be here all week!). You may be groaning now but you will never forget this important truth that so many churches overlook. This is the truth that transformed my life and ministry! Many congregations and youth pastors spend the majority of their time caring for caught fish in the tank instead of heading out into the oceans that are teeming with uncaught fish.[13] That is where Jesus wants to take us if we dare to let him climb aboard to redirect our journey and calling. We are destined for deeper waters! Some churches and youth ministries actually fight over the few fish that are already caught and miss the millions out in the oceans. In my home of San Diego County, for example, there are over 400,000 middle and high school students in public schools alone. Public schools are the last place left in our culture where everyone gathers on a regular basis. God has provided an incredible opportunity for churches if we can learn to love and serve students and schools well.

As mentioned earlier, "mission work" for churches does not always need to involve crossing the Pacific or Atlantic Oceans. It can also happen by simply crossing the street and coming alongside a public school in meaningful ways. Several years ago, a principal from Crawford High School in San Diego told a pastoral colleague of mine that they have one student from every country in African represented in their student body of approximately 1,600 kids. In America's cities, the nations have literally come to us. As a church, are we willing to go to them? This is the challenge Jesus issues to the church when he calls Peter to fish differently and become the leader of his new movement.

Immediately Peter left his boat to follow Jesus. He began catching dead people so they could become alive again. *That type of fishing makes for a much more rewarding vocation than catching living fish that die quickly because they met you.* Nothing is more exhilarating than watching kids in front of their friends, in a student-led public school club, raising their hands saying "I want Jesus in my life." That's the best. It can't be beat!

This brings me to an important point in our conversation. I believe lost people still really are lost. Today is it easy to find modern theologians, denominations, professors, and pastors who believe hell could not possibly exist, or that it is not forever, or that all people are indirectly saved from eternal punishment regardless of their specific beliefs and practices as long as they are "sincere" about them. Unending suffering seems unjust to certain thinkers since people commit sin in finite time and space. The atonement of Christ itself, others argue, is a barbaric and brutal act unnecessarily conjured up by a bloodthirsty and vengeful deity. Yet when we take Jesus at his words and actions, it becomes clear from scripture that payment for sin is absolutely necessary. Thankfully, God made a way for human guilt to be covered when he sent his son, as the perfect lamb, to take on the punishment we all justly deserve.[14] People still need others to go after them so they can be found, experience forgiveness, come to salvation, and enjoy life to the fullest in Christ.

All the committees and scholars in the world can write and vote all they want, but they cannot change the universal pull that both gravity and depravity have on the human race. Well-written books, articles, lectures, or opinions cannot alter our need for a savior. Jesus came to Peter with the task of fishing with an urgency that compelled him to "seek and save" the lost because they actually *needed* it. We all do.

Jesus was – and is – passionately recruiting disciples to join in a life and death enterprise. Otherwise, he was a fool to go through all the suffering and torture he endured on the cross if everyone is alright to begin with. I can hang up my sneakers now if I could suddenly declare – as some North American theologians have – that lost people no longer need saving. Indeed, even though it is not up to me, making such a declaration would be much easier. Now that I have finished a Ph.D. in Religion from Claremont Graduate University, I have definitely run into scholars – and church leaders – who want to convince me that my job as an evangelist is no longer theologically necessary in the 21st Century. My life certainly would require less effort if my friends who see these matters differently are right. If I believe them, I would not have to preach hard on the weekends, raise close to a million dollars a year, empower young people, or equip churches to support student leaders on campuses. But I don't think that is the conclusion Jesus, or the scriptures, come to about the lasting hunger, enduring problem, and eternal potential built into human existence. Holding an iPhone does not change this universal truth about every human. As people made in God's image, we are all invaluably worth going after, finding, and catching in order to experience Jesus' exhilarating new reorientation of our lives.

Whoever Gets There First Wins

Several years ago, I was at Lincoln High School setting up the lights for a motivational assembly our organization hosted for all sophomores on campus the following day. After setting up the presentation with the principal, everyone involved looked forward to getting out of class for a time of inspiration. When I arrived to set up the lights with the facilities crew, however, I was surprised to see another group rehearsing their assembly. They had a banner that read, "Helping Southern California People Make Healthy Choices." They had professional backdrops with video monitors mounted into the artistic frame which stretched across the entire length of the stage. I watched as a young twenty-somethings group performed a well-choreographed dance routine. I thought to myself, "This is compelling art, I wonder what their message is?" Halfway through the presentation, I found out the answer. Two of the dancers got closer together while other members of the team ran off stage and came back carrying a big banner with one word written on it: Condom. Yes, this story is rated PG-13, but scenes like this happen quite often in America's public schools. They then proceeded to wrap the two dancers together in this large roll-up sign as their team carried the newly joined couple offstage into the shadows. Meanwhile, bottles of KY Jelly lubricant appeared on the video monitors and shook back and forth as the two teenagers continued to linger backstage. That was the school's message for every freshman in my neighborhood two months into their high school career. "Welcome to ninth grade," the program non-verbally announced, "we know you are going to make bad decisions anyway, so just take precautions." Sex is much more significant than biology; whether teenagers know it or not, a permanent spiritual bond takes place. As my mentor Duffy Robbins says, "There are no condoms to protect the heart."[15] I wish this life-changing truth got dispensed into the lives of more young people in my community.

Toward that end, we also had an interactive multi-media presentation prepared for all sophomores on Tuesday of that same week. The group described above beat me by a grade level and by a day. They got to all freshman on Monday – an audience of six hundred kids – before we did. But we have a very different message. "Your life is worth more than you can imagine and there is greatness in you that needs to be developed and set loose. Don't settle for less." We want each young person to finish their story. We know God wants to write it. That's the message that we promote in assemblies. But whoever gets there first, wins the conversation.[16]

As I contemplated urban ministry during my undergraduate years, I read a copy of *Newsweek* magazine with Eugene Rivers on the cover. He is an inner-city pastor in Boston who, at the time, helped pioneer a coalition of clergy that worked alongside cops to curb gang violence on the streets of his community. I later got to meet Reverend Rivers personally during my divinity school days in New England. I still remember a part of the article where he recounts the first conversation he had with one of the main drug dealers in the neighborhood soon after Rivers moved in. As a new pastor on the block, Rivers asked him why gang members and drug dealers were more successful than churches when it comes to capturing the imaginations and loyalties of neighborhood young people. The seasoned drug dealer and gang member replied from his experience, "I'm there when Johnny goes out for a loaf of bread for Mama. I'm there, you're not. I win, you lose. It's all about being there."[17] That was the message this pastor got from the underground economy about how they recruit students. Incarnational ministry – "being there" – works whether you play for the kingdom of darkness or the kingdom of light. It's a basic law built into the universe of human relationships. Whoever gets there first usually wins. If a person is starving and somebody offers them junk food, they are going to take it because that is still far better than dying of hunger. They may not have tasted the bread of life – God's word and love – that satisfies the soul and does not leave you emptier and more ashamed afterwards. We will all keep trying to appease our appetite with other things until we meet Christ. As Saint Augustine said so well, "Our hearts are restless till they rest in Thee."[18]

I left that assembly program with a righteous anger boiling inside, saying to myself, "I want to get there first." I want to be better funded than those guys. I want to beat the other voices in youth culture at their own game. I want to get there before the other influencers. I want to be more authentic, more consistent, more accurate, more sacrificial, more predictable, and stay longer than the other voices. Kids will listen to whoever makes it there – and stays there – first. And then they will usually follow whoever gets there first regardless of whether that voice is leading to life or to death. Nothing beats the exhilaration of getting there first to share words of Jesus leading to resurrection life.

More Rejoicing Over One Than Ninety-Nine

I did lose a kid on my shift at camp one summer. Our church was up at Forest Home, a large and beautifully expansive camp in the mountains near San Bernardino, California. That week, as the youth pastor, I had sixty-five middle school students under my care. After about four hours of free time, a volunteer came running up to me in the cafeteria with a look of panic across her face. "Markus [name changed] did not check in after free time," she told me. "No one knows where he is." I thought to myself, "Not on my shift." There's a lot of paperwork when you lose a kid up at camp. Plus, I really loved him. So I started asking around during dinner, "When did you see Markus last," "when did *you* see him last," "when did *you* see him last?" Three kids told me the same story. "We saw him in the creek playing down by the river bed," they said, "right before the flash flood washed through this afternoon." On rare occasions at this camp, storms can push a surge of water down from the mountains. It overflows the banks, floods the cabins, and then subsides as quickly as it came. Alarms, sirens, and flashing lights had all gone off that day to warn of the impending high waters. Cabins got flooded and some kids spent the rest of the day wringing out their clothes and belongings. So I knew these shared stories could definitely be true. Immediately, we all started looking for this lost kid. All of my staff put their forks and knives down and started canvasing the massive camp. The entire paid camp staff put their utensils down and started looking. No one filled out a spiritual gifts inventory to find out if they felt called to youth ministry, evangelism, service, the gift of helps, or search and rescue. They just knew this is a life and death emergency and we had to find this kid at all costs. We had to go get him and bring him back.

I started crying. I prayed some of my life's most sincere prayers as I walked all over the camp frantically looking for him. I knew I had about twenty minutes left before I had to call his mom. Can you imagine that conversation? "The kid you love and trusted me with, your own flesh and blood," I would have to say, "is lost on my shift." I had no idea where he was. As I considered this dreadful phone call, I got to the large bridge over the river that separates one section of camp from the other. I looked right. I looked left. I shouted Markus's name and listened to it echo in the mountains. As I surveyed the river, I prayed to God that I would not see a brown hump shaped like a junior higher washed up alongside the bank. But that's exactly what was going through my mind. The whole time, I was praying with all my heart. I tried to fight back more tears. I was dying inside. Nobody answered!

Finally, I got to the center of the camp and arrived at the bookstore. I knew I had about five minutes left before I had to call his mom. Just then, the double doors of the bookstore suddenly burst open and this groggy-eyed kid, Markus – the one we were looking for – comes staggering out. I ran to meet him. I could not help myself.

Now I'm usually an appropriate side-hug, I-love-you-but-I'm-not-getting-sued kind of youth pastor. But when I saw this kid who was possibly dead and is now alive, who was lost and now found, I lost all composure and I just sprinted to him. I picked him up and I pulled him close. I said, "Markus, you don't know how good it is to see you." (I think I really scared him). "What happened?" I asked. "I found a really good comic book *series* and lost track of time," he told me. "I have been reading in the book-store for the last four hours." Now when you work with kids that are tempted by gangs, and drugs, and endure neighborhood homicides, as long as they're alive, it's a good thing. So for me, he could have said anything. He could have said, "I was sampling crystal meth for the first time in the camp bookstore." I would have said, "Markus, I don't support that kind of behavior but at least you're still here and we can work on it together." There is always time to make a wrong decision right if you are still alive.

I was so overjoyed at having him back that I literally threw him onto my shoulders when we got back to the cafeteria. When we entered the room together, there was more rejoicing over the one junior higher that was lost than over the sixty-four others that never needed to be found again. It was exhilarating! That's what fishing for men and women is all about. That's the joy of seeing the lost come home again.

The Only Hands and Feet of Jesus Today

We all have a role to play in reaching the next generation. We have all received the baton of faith and it is our job to pass it on to those coming after us. The point of receiving the baton is not just to faithfully run your race but to pass it off to the next leg. Receiving the baton comes with the responsibility and privilege of successfully passing it forward. That's the point of receiving it. That's what it is for. Could you imagine a runner in the Olympics who receives the baton only to become captivated with how bright and shiny it is? Then, how absurd would it be if the runner decides to keep it safely tucked into his spandex uniform so it will never be harmed and no one will take it away? That would be crazy! The reason we receive our faith in Christ is so we can pass it on to those who follow after us. Regardless of how young or old we are as saints, Jesus has a role for us to play. We all have received time, talent, treasure, and truth. Therefore, we all have the privilege and responsibility to relay them successfully to, and put them to work for, the next generation.

I once heard a pastor talk about an inner-city church that kept getting tagged with spray paint and vandalized repeatedly. People continued breaking in, damaging, and disrespecting their sacred space. This left the congregation feeling understandably upset and violated as vandals messed with the inside and outside of the church. Each time, the congregation paid for the repairs and kept fixing the damages as they occurred. One week, the ultimate insult happened. When the congregation arrived for mass on Sunday, they saw the statue of Jesus – with his arms outstretched, look-ing over the community – standing in its usual place. Except this week, the vandals had the audacity to break the hands of Jesus off at the wrists. They were gone! Who does that? So the church held another business meeting with members in order to decide what to do. Initially, they planned to fix everything just like they had previously. But then, in the back, an older saint spoke up and said, "I have a better idea." Then she went on to describe her plan which the congregation eventually accepted. When everyone came back for worship the next week, they saw that Jesus was still there, his arms still outstretched, and his hands were still missing. But there was a new plague at the base of the statue that had not been there before. It read, "I have no hands but yours."[19] That's a pretty good way to remember the point of going in and going out of church each week. We are the only hands that Jesus has left on Earth. If we don't go out and love people, high five people, embrace people, give, serve, or surrender our lives, and point people to Jesus, then those actions will not happen. We now are the body of Christ. In many cases, the only Jesus someone else will see is you or me! There are no hands to reach out and carry the next generation except us. There are no hands now, but yours…and mine. Let's pass the baton.

God Left Us Here on Purpose

When I was in junior high, I got misplaced as a sound engineer in the back of a storefront church in Lancaster, Pennsylvania. Today, I have great respect for the audio/visual guy who can effectively run the sound system without disruptions while I preach. That was not me back in middle school. I had no idea what I was doing. I was "in training" and flying shotgun in the co-pilot chair while the main technician tried to teach me the ropes. One morning, the sermon was particularly good and caught my attention as I sat back at the sound board. The preacher was talking about Jesus coming back one day. You may have heard a sermon like this before. He got his rhythm going and I started getting into it. He kept saying, "At any given moment, the trumpet might sound, the clouds might part, and Jesus will come back to take us all up with him." I was so into the sermon that I lost track of the fact that the reverb dial

— the echo knob on the sound board — was at about a nine-and-a-half. Usually it's supposed to be about a one or a two. If you run sound at a Pentecostal church, you can get away with having the dial turned up to a three or a four. Nine-and-a-half is never good. Nonetheless, this preacher kept preaching and finally said, "This might be your last moment before Jesus comes back and, in a twinkling of an eye, takes us all up to be with him." At that very moment, I kid you not, my knee accidentally hit the sound board. The entire storefront church heard a huge bang from above followed by strange loud vibrations echoing throughout the room… and everybody looked up. The pastor stopped and looked up too. And eventually everyone looked back down. Then they realized that the pastor was still there. Elder John was still there too… and rumor has it he was a regular tither. Then in unison, they all turned around and starred back at me. Suddenly they figured out that it was a sound engineering problem. All I could do was shrink in embarrassment because I was the junior high sound boy who inadvertently faked the rapture on a Sunday morning.

Why do I tell you all that? I tell you that because God has left us here on purpose. If Jesus is God and the Father can send him back at any time he wants, he could have sent Jesus back when I was in junior high. God could do it before you finish reading this next sentence. He could have done it when the late radio broadcaster Harold Camping put up thousands of billboards across the country incorrectly announcing that the rapture was scheduled for May 21, 2011. He seemed more interested in raising large sums of money by predicting the rapture than he was concerned about spending it to care for people.[20] But Jesus is all about people. God hasn't sent Jesus back yet because, if he did so now, many people in my city and yours would be eternally separated from him forever.

Since I earned a Ph.D. in religion and ethics, people sometimes ask me how a loving and all-powerful God could allow tsunamis, divorces, mass murder, poverty, war, depression, injustice, cancer, human trafficking, loneliness, (Justin Timberlake concerts,) and other painful events instead of just coming back and fixing everything now. As tragic as some circumstances are – and as deeply as they break God's heart every time – I believe he allows the sun to come up one more day because he is hoping more of his people decide to be the hands and feet of Jesus. Who else will go out to love and serve a hurting world? Who will pass the baton to one more person?

To Jesus, the only pain more excruciating than all the daily brokenness on planet Earth, is the thought of spending eternity apart from the kids that he loves so desperately. That's why God allows the sun to come up again on another day before ending the current age and sending Jesus back. If you and I wake up "unraptured" tomorrow morning, it is because God has put us here on purpose. You could be placed nearby one more person who needs to be loved, to experience God's kingdom, and be brought into the fold of the family of God. When that happens, there is more rejoicing over the one that was lost than over the ninety-nine that never need to be found again.

t w o

A PACIFIST FARM BOY
FIGHTS FOR URBAN KIDS

My unexpected call to urban ministry shows that God definitely has a sense of humor. I grew up as a white mid-western boy in rural Michigan who lived along a dirt road, with corn rows growing beside my house. Long before any of my experiences with diversity in US cities, I had no idea that corn rows could actually be a hairdo. I had lots of important lessons to learn. God would eventually transport me from the corn rows I knew and introduce me to new ones found on the heads of my African American brothers and sisters. God enjoys taking themes from our past and repurposing them so they are infused with fresh meaning. That is what he does best through his creative and regenerating work in our lives.

By the time I hit my adolescent years, I found myself caught deeper in the type of corn rows I originally grew up with. I ended up picking ears of sweetcorn for minimum wage on a farm near my family's new home in Lancaster County, Pennsylvania. This region is the same place that inspired music parodist Al Yankovic's song "Amish Paradise" because of the high concentration of conservative, plain-dressing Anabaptist farmers who drove horse-drawn buggies across the beautiful country landscape. As conservative Mennonites – theological cousins to the Amish – my parents grew up in this unique community and returned to raise me with some of the same values they had inherited from their culture of origin. Dotted with windmills, covered bridges and lush green fields, going to middle and high school there was like living in a picturesque time warp. I literally drove my Honda civic past horse-drawn Amish buggies on the way to class every day. Back then I never dreamed that God would take me from "Amish paradise" to – what some may consider to be – a "gangsta's paradise" in southeast San Diego.[21]

While gang-related homicides have dropped in my neighborhood over the past decade, my wife and I raise our three young children (and three foster daughters) in a section of town where weekend shootings remain all too common. As I sit and write today, reporters are covering another fatal gun incident that took place in our community two days ago.[22] During my teenage years, my parents sent me to a Mennonite school and raised me to be a pacifist – and a registered conscientious objector – as far as violence and war are concerned. On my eighteenth birthday, when it came time to register for the draft, I filled out the card by writing the following message, "I am a conscientious objector to war of all types." At the time, I never planned on entering an urban war zone to fight for the well-being of kids – both spiritually *and* literally in some cases. In an eternal sense, I have found one type of warfare that I cannot afford to remain uninvolved with or indifferent to. A *pacifist*, as illustrated in the movie *Hacksaw Ridge*, needs not be *passive* when it comes to saving the lives of others in danger. The battle we engage in for young people, however, is spiritual in nature and never ends. In this war, I have been called to fight and recruit others to join me on the front lines. Together we can all pray the same prayer from that movie, "Please, Lord, help me get one more. Help me get one more."

War rages every day for the young people I love in our community. Every soul is a battleground.[23] As I continue to grow – still nourished by my Mennonite roots – I now consider myself to be a "Presbycostal" who believes spiritual realities manifest themselves in physical, relational, and systemic conflicts. Since starting UYC nine years ago, I have attended. and also officiated, more than my fair share of funerals for teenagers who died way too young, often under tragic and senseless circumstances. Some of those stories appear in the pages that follow. Through it all, I decided that if I am unwilling to pick up a gun to defend those I love, then I must learn to fight for the well-being of teenagers in my city through other means. The apostle Paul said it well in 2 Corinthians 10:4-5 when he writes:

> For the weapons of our warfare are not of the flesh but have divine power to destroy strongholds. We destroy arguments and every lofty opinion raised against the knowledge of God, and take every thought captive to obey Christ.

Since the battle we fight is ultimately not against flesh and blood, but against principalities, powers, and spiritual forces of evil in the heavenly realms (Ephesians 6:12), it makes sense that our main weapons will not come from an earthly arsenal. Since a true spiritual battle wages for every life, we must enter into the battle through prayer, fasting, proclaiming scripture, worship, acts of service, works of justice, welcoming the stranger, loving everyone regardless of their response, and faithfully retelling Jesus' words of resurrection life. God's armor of light equips us to stand our ground when the battle escalates around us and those we care about most.

When Jesus founded the church through the apostle Peter, he promised that the gates of hell shall not prevail against her.[24] This language is important because hell's gates refer to protective and defensive structures. Therefore, we can assume Jesus intends his church to be on offense – acting together to storm the fortress of hell and set captives free. From this perspective, we discover that our primary enemy is not a neighborhood gang member, a secular school district, a local drug dealer, an overwhelmed coach, classroom bullies, a family member with personal pain, calculating politicians, or any other person or system. Ultimately, the enemy we fight is the enemy of all human souls. He holds many kids and adults in our society captive. We want to see them set free by the truth, carried off by God's irresistible love, and pardoned by divine forgiveness through Jesus. Then, they too can join Christ in the mission of seeking and saving the lost and brining about more of God's kingdom on earth as it is in heaven.

Strength Made Perfect in Weakness

After two decades of ministry in the cities of Philadelphia, Boston, and San Diego, Jesus has now *made me into* an effective fisher of men and women within an urban context. I want to see students experience life to the *fullest* from Jesus in every sense of the word.[25] Academically, this means good grades at a successful school with a connection to a future in college or other vocational opportunities. Physically, this means having healthy food, clothes, shelter, safety, and access to medical care and the basic necessities of life. Spiritually, this means discovering a relationship with Jesus

Christ that has the power to completely transform a person, entire families, and eventually whole neighborhoods, both now and for-ever. Economically, this means getting the opportunity to become employable in a profession that provides dignity, purpose, and joy while also supporting a family and making a positive contribution in the world. Socially, this translates to meaningful friendships, relationships of justice, and belonging to a cohesive family that loves and accepts us. While teenagers may attend a school named after a US president in my city or yours, too many young people who walk its halls feel like the elusive American dream is pass-ing them by. My passion is to awaken young people to a bigger *kingdom* dream for their lives which empowers them to overcome obstacles and beat long odds with supernatural strength.

When Moses first heard God's call to deliver the children of Israel from slavery in Egypt, he protested saying he was not a good enough speaker.[26] He quickly pointed to his stuttering problem as proof that he was unfit for the job. Like Moses, I first thought it would be impossible for God to use me because of who I am. My physical problem was not speaking, however, it had to do with hear-ing. I told God that I was too deaf to be used in a meaningful way. From birth, I have been 100% deaf in my right ear and have 20% hearing loss in my left ear as well. I now wear a hearing aid in my "good" ear to pick up as much lost sound as possible. Growing up, I often felt insecure in group settings because I frequently missed important things others said to me. One time, a fellow classmate came up to me midway through the school year and apologized for "hating" me. I asked her why she had such strong feelings against me since we rarely talked to each other. She went on to explain that whenever she called out my name to greet me, I would stare straight ahead – with a deadpan expression on my face – and walk past without acknowledging her presence. Since it appeared as if I was purposely ignoring people, she concluded that I must be conceited, viewing myself as better than everyone else at school. Once she found out I was deaf, she felt horrible about the animosity she harbored against me.

I quickly forgave her. But a lingering question remained in my mind. How could God use me effectively in cross-cultural relationships if my hearing loss created so many problems relating to people in my own community who have the same skin color and background as me? Like Moses, I not only had a physical handicap, but as a white man aspiring to do urban ministry, I initially felt like I had a cultural handicap too. "They will surely reject me," I thought. "What do I have in common with their stories?" I asked. Moses also knew that he would be in an awkward position should he answer the call of God and return to Egypt. As an outlaw wanted for murder, he had thrust himself deeply into the divide between the Hebrews and Egyptians by killing a slave master who mistreated an Israelite laborer. Torn between two cultures, he knew both sides would be reluctant to receive him back due to his sketchy past and dual identity. He felt caught in no man's land, a hybrid who struggled to fit in anywhere. He had nowhere to call home except the wilderness where God met him.

When God asks Moses, "What is in your hand" he directly addresses this dilemma by pointing out the wandering convict's shepherd's staff.[27] This tool which Moses carried was only used for the profession of sheep herding, which Egyptians despised.[28] A true prince of Egypt would never carry one. It signified his source of greatest shame and the fact that he was a castaway out on the run. Moses may have even used this staff, or one similar to it, to kill the slave master that got him exiled from Egypt forty years earlier. By asking for his staff, God challenges Moses to lay down his past mistakes, identities, and insecurities. This act of trust and surrender allows God to transform it into something new and extraordinary – a serpent. Through this scary act of faith, Moses trusted God enough to pick it up again with renewed meaning and power – and it became a staff once again. In that moment, God forever changes Moses, his staff, and his story. The very thing Moses was most ashamed of became the instrument that God uses to bring down the world's most powerful empire at that point in human history. All the miracles of deliverance and liberation in the Exodus account took place through Moses' transformed shepherd's staff. His greatest source of brokenness, weakness, and shame became the vehicle of God's greatest power to rescue millions of lives.

Fortunately, God often calls people first, then does some of the equipping later on. His "on the job training" even makes use of – and repurposes – experiences from a person's past. He can turn weaknesses and previous failures into assets, especially for people who think they have nothing to offer or something in their past that would disqualify them. Much like trading in my old corn rows for new ones, God took my deafness and turned it into an advantage in cross-cultural relationships. Being partially deaf forces me to listen carefully to others and to approach every new person and community from a posture of vulnerability, humility, weakness, and respect. It constantly requires me to be interdependent with others who can help me notice what I might be missing. This is a great principle for life and ministry. Much of my work now consists of leading teams so that we can hear and respond to God's voice together, more than we ever could alone. In every encounter and conversation, I must rely on Christ's power to work through my brokenness. It serves as a constant reminder that I am dependent upon listening for God's voice above all other voices. Through the gift of weakness, Jesus leads me and demands my attention on a daily – sometimes minute by minute – basis. I have learned, as the apostle Paul did, to fully appreciate my weaknesses. In 2 Corinthians 12:9-10, he writes:

> But he said to me, "My grace is sufficient for you, for my power is made perfect in weakness." Therefore I will boast all the more gladly of my weaknesses, so that the power of Christ may rest upon me. For the sake of Christ, then, I am content with weaknesses, insults, hardships, persecutions, and calamities. For when I am weak, then I am strong.

Through my limited hearing, God gave me a constant reminder of my dependence on his unlimited power. I cannot fool myself into thinking I can do things alone. I need to endlessly enlist others so we can respond together as God speaks and leads us.

Since that day God spoke to me beside the McDonalds across the street from San Diego High School, he has done a mighty work in our city and county. A coalition of fifty-six churches now supports student-led Christian clubs and motivational assemblies at over one hundred middle and high school campuses in San Diego County and Mexico. In San Diego, these student-led meetings draw over 3,300 kids who enjoy physical and spiritual food every week. This safe and legal space becomes sacred ground where young people talk about Jesus with friends who may not see or experience kingdom relationships being lived out otherwise.

Only after completing an undergraduate degree in sociology and youth ministry and all my years of seminary did I discover it was legal for students to lead Bible club meetings on public school campuses in America. This important fact was not included in my undergraduate training nor my Master of Divinity courses in graduate school. My doctoral courses in Religion did not cover this material either. If kids start a Christian club at their school that is student led, voluntarily to attend, and meets during non-instructional time (before school, lunch, or after school), young people can gather their friends and invite a youth pastor as a guest who serves physical and spiritual food, all while convening on a public school campus. Although regular access to healthy food is a big problem in our city, students are hungry for more than the burritos and pizza at these meetings. Whether they know it right away or not, deep inside they are hungry for the bread of life found in God's word and in Jesus himself. Unapologetic, student-led evangelism can be blended with an approach that meets practical and holistic needs at every turn. As a goal, we work hard to exemplify the apostle Paul's exhortation that, "If possible, so far as it depends on you, live peaceably with all."[29] We work intentionally to avoid all unnecessary offenses that come with following Jesus while adding real value to the lives of the young people and the campuses we touch… As we will see in the pages that follow, this can take the form of motivational assemblies for thousands of students, grocery gift cards for hungry families, banquets for football teams, crises responses for youth homicides, school beautification projects, youth-led community service initiatives, and much more.

Before she passed away from lymphoma nine years ago, my mom, Dr. Jean Landis, came out to California to visit a student-led faith club firsthand. She heard what I had been describing and she wanted to see it for herself. On the day she arrived as a guest, about twenty seniors spontaneously came forward to request prayer because graduation loomed right around the corner. During this poignant moment, seniors asked for God's guidance, protection, and blessing as they stepped out into the unknown and uncertain future. As a strong Christian, my mom was both stunned and encouraged. She, too, was amazed that all this was possible and legal in a public school. Although she received a doctorate in education from the University of Pennsylvania – among the best universities in the field of education available in the US – her ivy league training never exposed her to the religious freedoms that public school students possess that make clubs like those described here possible. Little did we know that those civil liberties would come under direct attack by one of the largest school districts in California in the fall of 2015. Our network of congregations that support Christian student leaders and clubs grew to the point that the enemy would soon work very hard to take us out. More shots got fired in the urban war zone. This time they were aimed straight at our ministry and came from California's second largest public school district: San Diego Unified.

three

SHOTS FIRED BY CALIFORNIA'S SECOND LARGEST SCHOOL DISTRICT

The drama began with an unexpected text message from a high school principal in San Diego Unified School District (SDUSD) during the fall of the 2015-2016 school year. "Nate, can you call me?" was all his simple-but-cryptic message said. Since we worked together to bring five motivational assembly presentations to his student body the previous semester, I thought he may want to explore that possibility again. A few minutes later, we were on the phone together.

"Did you see the email?" he began.

"No," I responded. "What email?"

My mind started racing as I tried to guess what this might be about.

"You are part of the Urban Youth Collaborative, aren't you?" he continued.

"Yes, I am," I replied. I do not know if he realized I was the founder and President of the organization. At this moment, however, my title or job description did not matter at all.

"The district just sent an email out about you guys. It went to every middle and high school principal."

My heart sank.

The biggest school district in San Diego County, second largest in all of California, and eighth largest in the nation, decided to take on our ministry by name.

"This looks like an attack," he continued, "There are groups that can give you legal support for stuff like this."

A rush of different emotions washed over me as I tried to piece together what was happening. I wondered what all this was about. I felt afraid, confused, and even a little bit angry. After all the good we had done for kids over the past eight years, why were they acting against us behind our backs?

"I'll send it to you if you don't mind a long text message," the principal offered. He explained that the district can trace emails sent from their official servers and administrative addresses. He preferred to get it to me privately. I told him I understood and appreciated his help.

Throughout that week, several other principals began leaking the same troubling document to me and other members on our team. These, too, came from private email accounts and personal text messages. One principal even sat one of our staff members down in his chair so he could read the computer screen without having to resend it in any traceable way. The district's high priority email to all middle and high school principals – relayed by each of their six area superintendents – began this way:

It has been recently brought to our attention that there is a network, called Urban Youth Collaborative or UYC, that has been accessing our students through our ASB student religious clubs and engaging in religious activities which are not permitted by law, specifically "leading and recruiting."

The inaccurate "hit-piece" email continued by improperly alleging:

> Based on reports we have received, we are concerned that the UYC may be leading and recruiting new student members which is illegal. We are also concerned that District staff who are members of the churches involved with UYC may be assisting in this effort; though they may be unaware their actions are improper.

The malicious message campaign went on to quote our website out of context and provide administrators with a list of every campus where our organization supports a student-led faith club. They also included the names of every church youth pastor that supports students on each campus. All of this came directly from our organizational website. Principals could easily see who was being invited as guests at each school. This amounted to a "search and destroy" directive from a powerful-yet-misinformed few at the highest levels of the district. Our coalition of churches and the student-led Christian clubs we supported had grown to over eighty-three campuses throughout San Diego County and connected thousands of students each week. These statistics, which they copied from our website, created quite a stir that fall. The final paragraph of the district's first email required an immediate response by the close of the same business day from all campus site leaders who received it:

> We need you investigate and advise whether you have a religious club on campus that may be engaged in illegal religious

recruitment. In some cases, they may be leading lunch meetings led by an adult affiliated with the UYC network and serving pizza. Please visit this page [link to UYC's website provided] to identify the individual/individuals associated with the organization for your site. If you believe this or a similar organization is operating on your campus, please advise your area superintendent, Quality Assurance, and ████████████, General Counsel.

After faithfully, holistically, legally, and productively serving SDUSD students for over eight years, our coalition of churches had become a fresh target overnight. At first, we struggled to uncover the reason for such a sudden and aggressive district-wide "investigation." Even though I met the superintendent personally on two occasions – one encounter in which she thanked us for our school beautification work – their chief lawyer began acting as if we were terrorist cells that administrators needed to seek out and eradicate. After receiving and resending the overly-aggressive email as ordered by senior management, one area superintendent began referring to us as a "cult" in front of the principals she supervises.

Despite the negative responses of some district leaders, our track record of good deeds built considerable goodwill and relationships of trust at many of the middle and high school campuses where we worked. By this point in the story, our church partners had inspired students to complete over 80,000 hours of a youth-led community service campaign, fed four varsity football teams every week, mobilized thousands of faith-based volunteers to beautify campuses, officiated funerals for families in crisis, gave out thousands of dollars' worth of backpacks and grocery gift cards to hungry kids, and received annual recognition from the Mayor's office for our work with young people.

The principals who knew us personally understood that we had a long history of successfully serving and enhancing the lives of students and families. Our friends and allies knew we could be trusted because we know the rules and play by the rules. A handful of anti-religious principals did use the district's message campaign as an opportunity to interrogate student leaders and youth pastors that attended clubs as lawfully-invited guests. This caused a "cloud of suspicion" to hang over the district whenever the topic of student faith clubs came up.

Like many large urban school districts, SDUSD has a high turnover rate among principals. This revolving door of leadership can create an atmosphere of fear for some administrators who think their job may be in constant jeopardy. Principals feel considerable pressure to steer clear of conflict with the district no matter how ridiculous its actions may be. High administrator turnover also means that leaders new at the helm of a school may not know the positive track record of faith-based groups like ours prior to the email attack that inaccurately "introduced" us to them. Needless to say, my staff and I went on quite a tour of principal meetings to clarify the facts and the law that semester. In an environment where certain school leaders fear losing their jobs, many are new to their posts, and the legal nuances of religious liberties in public schools remains a mystery to officials, SDUSD thought they had found the perfect place to attack our well-established, positive movement.

Through this process, I learned that – no matter how politically savvy, relationally strong, community service-oriented, nuanced in language, holistically balanced, or well-researched our approach was – my naïve goal of following Jesus *without* persecution in the public square proved impossible to achieve. While we made many friends over the years, we inevitably created some foes too. In this case, we drew a few new and powerful ones. As Paul writes to Timothy, "Indeed, all who desire to live a godly life in Christ Jesus will be persecuted."[30] Even when I do everything in my power to eliminate all unnecessary offenses that Christians have added to the gospel – and there are many that need to be removed – I am still left with the unavoidable reality that the cross of Christ remains offensive to some who do not like what Jesus stands for.

A Professional Lobbyist Mom Strikes Back

The story behind the district's attack took shape when a well-connected mom – who runs a professional lobbying firm in San Diego – filed a district-wide complaint against our ministry. Her experience as a press secretary in a former San Diego mayor's office allowed her to mobilize as much dissent as possible within her considerable sphere of influence. She knew at least one school board member personally and used her clout to rally political momentum against our ministry. The district's chief lawyer, too, listened with an empathetic ear. Her anti-Christian sensibilities, combined with only a general familiarity regarding the religious freedoms afforded to public school students under the law, made for an ideal alliance between the district's chief lawyer and a powerful disgruntled parent.

This upset mom-on-a-mission effectively went around town against us because her son visited the outreach Bible club at his middle school one day in September of 2015.[31] This campus faith club – in its fifth year of existence at the time – was in good standing with the school up until this point. The meeting began with an announcement about the Christian nature of the gathering and gave students the option of leaving before being exposed to content they might be uncomfortable with.[32] This middle school student had most likely missed the club's disclaimer spelling out the "pre-flight religious safety instructions." He failed to get off the plane before takeoff.

Midway through the club meeting, after realizing that the group had a Christian focus, this junior high student asked to leave without specifying that he wanted to exit for religious reasons. Students need to be free to voluntarily leave a faith club meeting at any moment. We all agree on this point. At the beginning of this school year, however, the vice principal at this particular campus requested that students stay in the classroom until the end of the period to prevent anyone from wandering unsupervised with pizza away from the main lunch area. The club was meeting in a room apart from the regular "food zone" and the faculty advisor happened to be absent on this particular day. To honor the request from the school's vice principal, then, an adult volunteer supporting the club told the young man he needed to remain in the room until the end of the lunch period. This prompted the student to go home and tell his parents that he was basically locked in a classroom by a bunch of religious fanatics and forced to pray to Jesus! In reality, there was a short prayer of thanks prior to the pizza being passed out, but no one was ever forced to join in the optional prayer time. Needless to say, this account did not go over well with this politically well-connected family which harbored strong negative feelings about Christians who "proselytize" – especially using such "coercive" tactics inside a public school during the day.

At any time and for any reason, a SDUSD parent can file a district-wide complaint about an incident on top of a regular school-level complaint. Ordinarily, the issue described above would have been worked out with the leadership of a specific campus. In this case, we promptly met with the principal to discuss what happened and propose a solution. As mentioned above, we all agreed that kids need to be able to leave voluntarily. Yet the school never owned up to the fact that their own vice-principal's request kept the young man in the room that day. Consequently, the Christian club at the middle school where the complaint originated was banned for over five months.

To put this overreaction in context, each school year SDUSD receives so many parent complaints – over one thousand in an academic year – that they recently created an entire new department called the "Quality Assurance Office" to handle them all.[33] Due to such a high quantity, parental complaints receive varying degrees of attention. On this one occasion, however, a few senior managers decided to launch a district-wide, defamatory "investigation" of all Christian clubs due to *one* parent complaint at *one* school after a single child had a misunderstanding on *one* day. Clearly certain complaints get more traction than others depending on the subject matter and how connected the parents are to district officials. One politically powerful mother with a public relations firm prompted SDUSD to target us overnight without speaking to our organization directly. We made multiple requests to meet the superintendent in person to resolve the issue, but the overtures were repeatedly denied. One high-ranking district ally confided that if a single parent complaint always resulted in all-principal emails, then all he would do all day, every day, would be to sit in his office and send all-principal emails. Our case was indeed "special."

A Secret Emergency Pastors Meeting

We quickly convened all pastors and youth pastors serving with us to support students on campuses for an emergency prayer and informational meeting. I had to let everyone know that they were now "marked" men and women since the district email campaign targeted each of them by name. Whoever orchestrated this email attack – and subsequent versions that followed – hoped to take our ministry out overnight by scaring administrators into running us off their campuses. Some principals did harass student leaders to make them feel as if their club was shrouded in controversy or scandal. During the first week of the incident, our organization's Facebook page received thousands of views more than average as our opponents turned their crosshairs on us. We met to pray, strategize, and receive input from our organization's lawyer.

Friends in High Places

Following the initial attack, almost all principals in the district allowed faith clubs to continue meeting and inviting guests, despite the persistent misinformation campaign launched against us by the school district. Altogether SDUSD sent three separate and detailed "all principal" emails about Christian clubs in the fall of 2015. Two of the three were exclusively about our organization, our staff, and church partners by name. A third one attempted to clarify the laws for faith-based clubs on public school campuses in general. Yet that one, too, stemmed directly from the district's newfound fight with our organization. Christian student leaders and youth pastors suddenly had a whole lot of explaining to do. For use during our clarifying conversations with young people, teachers, and school administrators, our attorney, Dean Broyles, provided a two-page bullet point summary of the law to everyone who wanted accurate information about the robust religious liberties afforded to students and their invited guests. More specifics on this appear below and in the appendix. Nonetheless, the district's chief lawyer continued to send all-principal emails making it sound like our organization and the student-led faith clubs we support at public schools were shrouded in illegality, danger, and intrigue.

She also refused to return our calls or emails in a timely manner. As mentioned earlier, many principals do not know the law with respect to Christian clubs on public schools, so they looked to the district's chief lawyer to guide them. Fortunately, despite the flow of misinformation and animosity, God is the one who fights our battles. Both the law and the LORD are clearly on the side of student-led clubs meeting and inviting guests.

Praying Circles Around the District Headquarters

During the height of SDUSD's battle against us, I read *The Circle Maker* by Mark Batterson. He challenges his audience to draw prayer circles around their biggest challenges and dreams, refusing to give up or leave the circle until God miraculously answers. So I began driving around the district headquarters of SDUSD, asking for God's kingdom to come and *his* will to be done on earth as it is in heaven. Ironically – or providentially some might say – the district headquarters sits only six hundred yards from my church where UYC operates. I do not know if the district's vocal minority who resisted us realizes this. In fact, we open our parking lot so district personnel can use it as an overflow area for important School Board meetings. All this was taking place right under the district's nose – almost right across the street! God truly does have a sense of humor.

What the Law Really Says

This next section may feel a little tedious. But stick with me since the material is important to understand when congregations venture into the waters of public school ministry. As you will see, both Christian students and the adults supporting them have considerable freedoms under the law. I hope you find this encouraging. Our students sure did.

The Equal Access Act, passed in 1984, requires public secondary (middle and high) schools that receive federal funding to provide "equal access" to all students that want to form non-curriculum related clubs on campuses. If one other non-curriculum related club is permitted to meet at a school, then all other student clubs must be allowed regardless of the club's religious, political, philosophical, or lifestyle focus. As soon as a school allows one non-curriculum club to exist, this creates a "limited open forum" where other student groups can form clubs based on their varied interests as well.[34] If school administrators decide to close all clubs and be equally prohibitive to every student group, then they could legally argue this constitutes equal treatment. Since diverse non-curricular clubs enrich students' lives in many ways, however, taking such an extreme stance often makes for an unpopular public relations move with students, parents, and the community. If a principal decides to "close" a previously open forum for the purpose of denying one particular student group the chance to meet, a judge would likely deem this to be discriminatory if the case went to court.

As part of their First Amendment right to free speech, public school students may form clubs under the Equal Access Act provided they are student led, voluntary to attend, and meet during non-instructional time (before school, during lunch, or after school). A faculty member may serve as an advisor and be present to provide oversight and ensure order and safety in the room. He or she, however, may not actively teach or lead a club meeting in their capacity as a school employee. Outside adults from the community – such as pastors, youth pastors, and church volunteers – may be guests at student club meetings provided that those adults do not "direct, conduct, control, or regularly attend activities of student groups."[35] When invited as a guest speaker within the context of a Christian club meeting described above, youth pastors may openly pray, share from the Bible, invite students to respond to their message, and inform listeners about optional off-campus church events in the community. All of these communication exchanges may happen if student leaders would like that information shared by the adult guest they invite.

When it comes to avoiding "regular attendance" by outside adults, the strictest stance a school can take is to require some sort of rotation in order to avoid being non-consecutive in their presence. A specific definition of the phrase "non-regular attendee," along with a planned rhythm for achieving it, can easily be negotiated with each site principal. Since many clubs have separate student leader meetings in addition to the large group gathering, a case can be made that "non-regular" attendance means skipping one of the two meetings offered every week. Many student leaders invite multiple church pastors to their clubs using a rotation of every-other-week or once per month depending on how many adult guests they would like to have involved. Whatever adult access policy a school adopts must be equally enforced between all student clubs and groups. All promotional and advertising opportunities afforded to other clubs must be offered equally to Christian clubs as well. As you can see, there are broad freedoms for students who want to talk about life's biggest questions from God's perspective. They can absolutely meet and invite youth pastors to join them as contributors to these life-changing conversations.

God Will Fight for Us (Exodus 14:14)

While most faith clubs in the SDUSD continued after our circuit of principal meetings, three Christian clubs remained illegally suspended. This happened during the first week of the district's first email campaign against us. We retained attorney Dean Broyles as our legal counsel. His firm, the National Center for Law and Policy (NCLP), specializes in constitutional civil rights and religious liberties cases. Dean generously agreed to represent Urban Youth Collaborative pro-bono (for free). He has a very successful track record when it comes to defending the rights of student-led faith clubs in San Diego County and throughout the country. Plus, he is a former youth pastor. Broyles wrote a very strong eighteen-page legal memorandum to SDUSD's chief lawyer and copied the entire School Board. It clearly explained the law with respect to students' well-established rights to conduct religious clubs and invite guests on campus. Broyles demanded that the district reopen all suspended clubs immediately. This well-researched letter cited relevant case law and included a copy of the district's defamatory email which several administrators leaked to us. They were probably surprised we had a copy of their "hit piece" email, a firm grasp of the law, and effective legal representation.[36]

After receiving the memo, the district quickly reinstated two of the three banned Christian clubs they had unlawfully suspended. Their top lawyer, however, continually refused to meet, return phone calls, or dialogue in a constructive way with our counsel. Since the matter was "under investigation" by the district, she continued to suspend the Christian club where the initial complaint took place while searching for more "dirt" on us at other schools. The district hoped to churn up negative reports from other principals in an effort to support her case.

As a "General Counsel" for SDUSD, the district's chief lawyer is required to be broadly knowledgeable about a wide variety of legal matters. As a general practitioner, however, she did not appear to possess expert-level knowledge when it came to the religious liberties of students on public school campuses. The emails she sent to principals (we received all three leaks from concerned administrators) contained – what our attorney considered to be – legal errors and factual inaccuracies. Some misrepresentations may have been intentionally presented for strategic reasons. Other errors were perhaps accidental. Nonetheless, the district's behavior reflected strong biases against kids in their care who hold Christian religious beliefs. In his twenty years of working with public school Bible club cases on a national level, Broyles told me that SDUSD's treatment of Christian students was by far the most discriminatory and hostile he has ever encountered.

On SDUSD's web site, they state a promise to "welcome all students from all faiths within our school community."[37] It is important for the district to remember that this commitment must also extend to include the freedoms of students professing the *Christian* faith within the community schools they oversee. The district has taken great strides to ensure that the rights of other student clubs and groups are protected. During the same semester that they privately and aggressively interrogated the network of student-led Christian clubs that we support, they simultaneously published every Gay-Straight Alliance Club meeting day, time, location, and faculty advisor on the district's official website to make sure LGBTQIA students find the resources, safety, and support that they need in district schools. During the subsequent 2016-2017 school year, the district took clear steps to prevent the bullying of Muslim students who felt threatened due to – what some consider to be – rising "Islamaphobia" in US society.

I commend SDUSD for supporting the rights of students from different backgrounds to gather together, express their unique and diverse views, and develop a supportive community. *I only ask that they extend this opportunity to all students in the district… including those interested in discussing issues of personal faith and religion from a Christian viewpoint.* It is important that students and adults from all backgrounds develop respect, sensitivity, and compassion for those who see the world differently and who may even disagree with them. How we treat those who disagree with us, however, says more about our character than how we treat our friends. Bullying is never an acceptable behavior toward others viewed as different for any reason. If principals or district officials specifically target student-led Christian clubs or their adult guests due to personal preferences, then they are engaging in the very acts of discrimination and bullying they work hard to prevent for other student groups.

Two Seventh Graders Stand Up to California's Second Largest School District

The student leaders of the Christian club where the complaint ensued did everything in their power to cooperate and give school officials the benefit of the doubt during their group's five-month suspension. Altogether, they submitted five separate club applications that got rejected during the 2015-2016 academic year. At first, the students were told they needed two faculty advisors instead of just one. Even though this is not required by law or by district policies, they dutifully recruited a second teacher and resubmitted the application. The second version of the application was declined because it did not appear on an "official school application" form. Interestingly, the students had been asking for an official club application form for several months and the school never provided it. Nonetheless, they cooperated and turned in the application again, this time on an official ASB club form which they finally received.

The third application was declined due to alleged grammatical problems, "spelling errors," and a few margin notes on the page. The school, therefore, requested a "clean copy." I am sure every other junior high club application district schools received came in displaying flawless grammar and penmanship (note my sarcasm). Nonetheless, the students persevered and turned in a revised version as requested. Each delay, by the way, cost the club several weeks as they reworked, resubmitted, awaited the results of the mysterious – and ever changing – approval process. Their fourth application eventually got turned down, they were told, because it looked as if some "adult handwriting" appeared on the page this time. The school then told them that only student handwriting could be written on club documents. The students quickly "fixed" that problem and turned in the fifth version of their paperwork. I was amazed at the resilience and perseverance of these seventh grade leaders! A few administrators hoped that they could exhaust them and run out the clock on the school year. But they turned in yet another version of their club paperwork.

When the fifth version of their application got denied, there was little doubt about what was really going on. This time, the word "Christian" had a line drawn straight through the proposed club name and the words "Jesus Christ" were crossed out of the purpose statement the students selected for their group. By this point, the student leaders and parents knew this was simple religious discrimination and therefore plainly illegal. Having exhausted all other avenues of resolution over the past five months and with the club indefinitely suspended, the students and their families asked our lawyer Dean Broyles – who they retained personally – to file a federal lawsuit against SDUSD for religious discrimination in violation of the Equal Access Act and the First Amendment. The district's chief lawyer continued to avoid contact and failed to resolve the problem despite requests from families that wanted the club reopened. The student leaders and their parents felt they had no moves left except to give up or sue the district.

Prior to officially filing the complaint (lawsuit) in federal court, the NCLP's Dean Broyles sent a final legal demand letter and a copy of the completed complaint to the district and school board two weeks in advance. This served as a courtesy to inform SDUSD of the families' intentions. After stalling for over five months and ignoring our lawyer's previous warnings that the indefinite club suspension violated federal law, the school and the district quickly reversed course in one week once they saw a lawsuit was imminent. After limited communication throughout the drama, the district's chief lawyer responded with a very short email stating that the club application had been suddenly approved and that the students could begin meeting again. They considered the matter "resolved" and "saw no need for further debate." What a relief! Unfortunately, it took the threat of a federal lawsuit before this large district finally did the right thing for their students who express Christian beliefs.

The legal victory at the middle school where the complaint took place set a big precedent for the rest of the district. Any anti-religious principals and district officials learned that they cannot be hostile toward, nor endorse, the faith claims students voluntarily make on campus. Furthermore, they learned that Christian students have equal rights to form clubs at public schools, invite guests of their choosing, discuss topics selected without state interference, and inform friends about other optional off-campus events which they could attend if interested. Some hoped this attack would succeed at getting UYC kicked off of – or greatly diminish our supportive role at – all middle and high schools in SDUSD overnight. Instead, it established a precedent that students and their guests have broad religious freedoms under the Equal Access

Act and the First Amendment.[38] As I write all this up almost three years later, our position is much stronger now than before the attack took place. God brings great good for many out of what a few meant for evil (Genesis 50:20).

If Christian Clubs Work in the Land of California, They Can Work Anywhere

I share the story in this chapter to encourage and challenge you. If our ministry strategy works in the land of California, where a few powerful district leaders tried repeatedly to take us out, then this can work *anywhere in the US*. Many people of faith across the country make the most of opportunities to support student leaders and engage public school kids on their own turf. But far more need to do so. I hope you find this inspiring and emboldening – regardless of whether you are reading this in a suburban or urban context. As you can see from our situation, students who want to stand for Jesus cannot be stopped. The only thing that can stop a young person from discussing their faith in a public school is timidity or a lack of knowledge. Once several bold seventh graders risked everything by standing up to the giant of the school district, they motivated countless other students throughout San Diego to do the same.

When working with a public school, we must respect the reality that we are invited into someone else's house. My friend and colleague Jeremy Del Rio runs a wonderful organization that brings art and mentoring back to public schools in New York City. He came up with the helpful analogy that – as guests at someone else's home – we must "respect the terms of the invitation." In other words, we cannot go rummaging through someone's closet upstairs when the family only intended us to share a meal with them at the

SHOTS FIRED BY CALIFORNIA'S SECOND LARGEST SCHOOL DISTRICT

dining room table. Analogously, when students or administrators invite us into their house, we must honor the boundaries of what they brought us in to accomplish together. We cannot add our agenda to what we promised to achieve. We must adhere to the law and keep our word. This makes our work together possible. As spelled out here, there is ample room for faith-based conversations in the limited open forum of student-led Christian clubs. As we will explore in the chapters that follow, there is also ample room for people of faith to add real value to schools in a myriad of other "non-religious" ways too. Good deeds and good will go together well with good news. At the end of the day, students and families must remember that – as community stakeholders – they are ultimately the shared owners of the public school "house" where they attend. At every opportunity possible, students of good will should calmly exercise their freedom of speech, engage in legal faith-based activities, and bless students from all backgrounds in as many different ways as possible. Churches can come alongside this effort and make countless contributions at every turn. The pages that follow share more of the adventure that can unfold.

The Window Might Close, But It's Wide Open Now!

UYC's attorney, Dean Broyles, became a good friend as a result of this ordeal. He normally charges $500 an hour when dealing with constitutionally sensitive cases about religious liberties and civil rights. I think I owe him about $100,000, should he wish to charge for his services. During the heat of SDUSD's false allegations of illegality against our ministry, we talked on the phone for an hour or two several times a week while formulating each response to their actions. This did not count hours he spent writing letters to the school board or attending meetings on our behalf. Thankfully, he agreed to represent us pro bono under two conditions: First, he wanted our coalition of youth pastors to make the most of every opportunity and share the gospel with students when invited on campus as their guests. Secondly, he wanted students to invite friends to churches if they do not have a local church home. Since we love to see both of these things happen, I knew the leaders we support would continue doing just that.

I will never forget what he said to me during that conversation, though. "This may be a battle, but I will help you get a win this time," he told me. "But a time is coming," he said, "when the laws of this country may change, and then I won't be able to help you win as easily anymore." Based on his experience with the national political and religious climate in our country, Broyles predicts that the Equal Access Act may be revised or revoked in the next five to ten years. At that point, the victory described in this chapter may not be possible anymore. While the doors are still open, please use the strategies laid out in this book to reach a lost generation that still needs Jesus. What Paul wrote to the church at Ephesus is relevant for American congregations today: "Look carefully then how you walk, not as unwise but as wise, make the best use of the time, because the days are evil."[39] I joke with people that UYC may one day stand for "Underground Youth Collaborative" if the persecution of Christians continues to increase in our land. We could keep our same acronym and logo, but our strategies may have to evolve. In the meantime, we have an unbelievable opportunity to share the love of Jesus with America's biggest unreached population: public school students. The Holy Spirit is blowing across our land and may just bring revival to our nation at our time of deepest need.

four

STUDENT LEADERS: THE CHURCH OF TODAY

When God moves in history, he often chooses to work through young people. The chief designer of the universe does not check ID to make sure someone meets minimum age requirements before choosing them for a significant mission. All he looks for is a receptive heart exhibiting child-like faith. In fact, Paul tells Timothy not to let anyone look down on him because he is young. Instead, the next generation is supposed to set the example for grown-up believers "in speech, in conduct, in love, in faith, in purity."[40] Revivals and social movements in the US and across the globe sprung from God revealing his dreams, passion, and vision to young people. Rosa Parks, for example, was the *second* person who refused to go to the back of the bus at the dawn of the US civil rights movement. While she deserves all the credit she receives for her courageous moral act, it was an African American teenager – Claudette Colvin, a student at Booker T. Washington High School in Montgomery, Alabama – who first defied the unjust laws of her day because she believed in the higher truth that made her equal. As a teenager who saw every human as an image bearer of God, she had the vision of a better society and risked everything to live it out.

As a pastor to young people, I want to call out their God-given dreams and visions for a better world. To accomplish this, I see myself like a football coach in many ways. While volunteering as a chaplain (spiritual life coach) for several high school football teams, there are many evenings when I want to jump out onto the field to make a tackle as the opposing squad races down the sideline to score a touchdown against us. And there have been many times when our team was getting blown out when I was tempted to do just that. I could dive out there and make the tackle! I would certainly make the evening news that night. But it would be my *last* game as a coach or chaplain *ever*. Why? Because as an adult, I am not allowed on the field in the same way that students are. I can coach with all my heart. I can plead with students. I can train them. I can pray with them. I can instruct, disciple, inspire, fund, and strategize with young people. But they are the ones in the spiritual game on their campuses. Their friends will be won or lost based on how they play *on* the field and *in* the game. That is the only spiritual scoreboard that matters in the end. Student leaders are the last hope for their generation. As with the first disciples, Jesus is sending them into the villages and towns and schools as his ambassadors who represent his kingdom.

When adults say, "Youth are the church of tomorrow," in one sense I agree with them, because they are one hundred percent of our future. Yet it is critical for churches to realize that young people are also the church *today*. If older pastors like me wait until a vague and undetermined future arrives before we give young people real leadership responsibilities, then we may not have many kids left in churches *tomorrow*. We need the energy, creativity, spontaneity, risk-taking, passion, vision, and inspiration that young people bring to the body of Christ when we connect in an *intergenerational* fashion. The old school and the new school need each other. I think age segregation is one of the overall problems with contemporary youth ministries in American churches. It regulates youth ministry to the toy department of human affairs and prevents young people from discovering and using their gifts to bless and pour new life into the broader body of Christ, their communities, and their world. Young people also need the wisdom, perspective, life-experience, and maturity offered by the "seasoned saints" (read: *older members*) of the church. We often end up telling kids they need to wait until heaven or until they are older before God can do anything significant with their lives. Churches inadvertently send this message by allowing just one "youth Sunday" a year for young people to be part of the larger body of Christ in meaningful ways. With all the waiting, it adds to the "in-between" feelings of meaninglessness, boredom, and uncertainty that already pervades adolescence. If the only worthwhile parts of life happen in the future, what are contemporary students supposed to dedicate themselves to today? Young people are hungry for a word from God *now*! They want to be part of something that matters. I believe the type of active discipleship that Jesus calls young people to is exactly what they – and their friends, families, and communities – are looking for. When Jesus declares himself to be the "resurrection and the life," he was not just speaking in the future tense, he meant that his present power to transform lives is available to those who step out in faith and believe today.[41]

Some scholars make the case that most of Jesus' twelve disciples were teenagers. They point out that only Peter and Jesus needed to pay the temple tax when collectors pressed Christ on the issue. Levitical codes require payment to be made for everyone twenty years of age and older. Since Jesus' agitators were satisfied when only two of the disciples paid the tax, one can infer that the rest of the group had not yet entered their twenties. This observation leads Greg Stier to humorously point out that "Jesus was leading a youth group with only one adult volunteer: Peter!"[42] Rabbis typically taught students who were adolescents and Jesus – standing in that tradition – would have been no exception. The amazing thing about Jesus' training regimen, however, is that he took the initiative and directly recruited followers instead of asking them to seek him out and apply. The initiative that Jesus took with, and the potential he saw inside of, young people ought to inspire all of us who follow his lead.

Students Lead Prayers for Peace at Lincoln High School

I have witnessed young people reach out to grab hold of their true leadership potential when difficult circumstances compel them to act. Several years ago, an altercation erupted between a campus police officer and students in the parking garage behind Lincoln High School. The event made the news after a play fighting incident escalated into a full-blown melee. Several kids went to the hospital due to pepper spray and the officer sustained a head injury. Distrust brewed on both sides as students and police accused the other of overreacting and instigating violence. Cascading reactions followed until they reached a flashpoint in the community. The following Monday, political, religious, educational, and law enforcement leaders of all stripes showed up. The ACLU, the Nation of Islam, San Diego's Police Department, Al Sharpton's

National Action Network, San Diego Unified School District officials, and local pastors all came out to voice their concerns. The most powerful voice that day, however, came from the students who scheduled an outdoor prayer rally before first period early that morning. They invited Pastor Archie Robinson, who has supported their on-campus Bible club for the past eight years, to address the group before they bowed in prayer (see picture in photo section).

While a row of news media trucks camped outside the school gate, students were asking for God's presence to camp inside the school grounds. Nearly three hundred students and community leaders joined hands together. Some administrators reluctantly decided to join in after first watching cautiously from the sidelines. The press did not cover this large prayer gathering. They seemed more interested in the earlier bad news about skirmishes between police and a smaller number of students. The students coordinating the prayer effort, however, knew the school needed *something* more than the grown-ups – or any human – could provide. The young leaders figured out the answer. They knew that God was paying attention to their prayers for peace, unity, forgiveness, and respect for those who are different.

When young people stand up to reclaim their school communities, God answers. As the book of James says, "The prayer of a righteous person has great power as it is working."[43] Fortunately, scripture does not put a minimum age requirement on this spiritual truth. *Righteous people come in all ages, sizes, colors, and backgrounds thanks to the work of Christ.* Students who cry out passionately to God can see mighty things happen in their schools and neighborhoods. Just a few months ago, a similar prayer movement broke out at Morse High School as described in the feature story box below.

COURAGEOUS STUDENTS LEAD OUTDOOR PRAYERS AT PUBLIC SCHOOL

After a series of fights broke out at Morse High School during the fall semester, a group of student leaders from the campus Bible Club organized an optional prayer circle in response.

On a November afternoon during lunch, over 150 students gathered to publicly invite God's presence and peace to cover their campus.

The principal asked for photos of the event so she could place one on the school's website. "After all we have been through," Dr. Cynthia Larkin remarked, "I challenge anyone who thinks student prayer is a bad idea to propose a better solution for our school."

The Power of Words

Waking up and going to middle or high school requires an act of courage most mornings. I have great respect for anyone who bravely enters into the fray of adolescent culture to make a few friends, learn something, and try to survive along the way. The social codes and competition can be difficult for any person — regardless of how self-assured they are — to navigate. I will never forget my first fateful day of junior high. I was a brand new kid from out of town trying to find my way in the world after my dad's job change moved our family across the mid-west from Michigan to Pennsylvania. As an insecure, pudgy newcomer with thick glasses and braces, I stepped into the brand new school sporting a modest afro. My heart was full of excitement and a little apprehension. It did not take long for a gorgeous girl to walk up to me, check me out from my forehead down to my sneakers, and then run away giggling. I thought to myself, "Not bad for a first impression. The stunning and popular girl noticed me." I found out later, though, that there was another new kid at this small private school that same year. He also had light eyes and blonde curly hair like me. He met the beautiful girl earlier at summer camp before the school year began. They planned to become a boyfriend and girlfriend "item" in the fall. She saw *me* and thought I was *him*. I found out later that she ran away giggling because she told her friend, "He looked good over the summer, what happened to him since then?" This represents information that an insecure seventh grade male is better off not knowing when it comes to his approval rating with the opposite sex. It hurt me deeply to know that I was dubbed unattractive before the final bell rang on day one.

After that encounter, I began to view myself differently. I wrongly concluded that I was unlovable and unattractive, particularly to women. This led me to get into some bad relationships later in life. If you believe you are worthless, then you will find other people to treat you that way. We have all heard the saying, "Sticks and stones will break my bones, but words will never hurt me." As someone who works regularly with young people, I could not disagree more. Sticks and stones will break my bones, but words will break my…heart! Broken bones take several months to heal, but a broken heart – or shattered self-image – can last a lifetime.

Human beings have been given a magical gift. The wand lies between your teeth and mine. The power to speak new things – both good and bad – into existence hinges on the tongue. We are the only species on the planet that uses words. Monkeys can learn sign language and gang signs. Dolphins use sonar and can harmonize melodiously. But they do not possess words. Humans are the only creatures, made in the image of God, endowed with the ability to create with our mouths. When God made the universe, he did not need power tools or construction crews. He simply said, "Let there be light," and "Bang!" billions of galaxies were born. He said, "Let there be land and sea, male and female, day and night," and it happened just as God said it should. People have the God-given power to create by speaking things into existence within the lives of others. She may not have known it or meant to, but that stunning girl in seventh grade looked at me and said, "Let there be a *loser!*" And she created one. I started living out the program that her words downloaded into my brain. Whether we know it or not, believe it or not, like it or not, we are all planting seeds in other people's souls every time we speak. Words have the power to sustain us or destroy us depending on what is packaged inside each seed.

With the words they use, kids chart a course for their lives during an impressionable and vulnerable season. When traveling for years, being off just one or two degrees results in a drastic change in our final destination. The book of James describes the tongue as the rudder on a ship that sails someone's destiny into the direction of life or death.[44] This is why I believe student gatherings in public schools are so powerful and life changing. They allow young people to speak words of resurrection life and hope to their friends who may be feeling broken, empty, lonely, hurt, or worthless.

Getting exposed to the right words instead of the wrong words can literally be a matter of life and death for students. Many years ago, one of the student leaders we supported felt alone and overwhelmed with the responsibilities of keeping his club going. As a linebacker on the football team and a junior filling out college applications, he had many responsibilities on his plate. Few students stepped forward to share the leadership burden. Even though the club was well attended and his teaching solid, he wondered if his "puffs of air" made any real difference week after week.[45]

So one day he prayed and said, "God, if you want me to lead this club again next year, you need to give me a sign." So the next week he got up in front of his friends, shared God's word with all his heart, and invited his friends to respond to the message. After he finished, a young female student sitting in the back came forward and said, "You don't know me because I don't talk very much when I come to this club. But because of this club, I now know that God loves me." She did not know that before.

Imagine going through your whole life not knowing that there is a God who loves you and has a plan and purpose for your time on earth. A great weight lifted off her shoulders when she realized the truth of God's personal love for her. Nothing could prepare Sam for what she said next. "Because I know God loves me, I have decided not to end the life of the baby that I am carrying inside me." She had not shared her situation with anyone before this moment. After hearing that, this young leader must have looked up at the the sky and said, "I was hoping for a more direct sign but this will have to do."[46]

God literally used this young man to save the life of two people that day – the mother and her beautiful baby girl. She went on to marry her boyfriend, join the leadership team at the school club (so Sam did not feel as alone), and became an active participant in the local church that supports student leaders at the school. Wow! Students can make a life-changing difference in the lives of others *right now* – not just when they are older.

Twenty Seconds of Outrageous Courage

I love the movie *We Bought a Zoo,* loosely based on the story of Benjamin Mee, a Los Angeles reporter who scrapped his old life to rehab a run down old zoo in Dartmoor Zoological Park in England. Toward the end of the movie, Benjamin's character – played by Matt Damon – takes his two kids to the coffee shop where he met his wife for the first time. As his kids stand attentively by, he reenacts the day he walked past the bay window and saw their future mom – the most beautiful woman he had ever seen – sitting there alone. According to the dad, all it takes to be successful in life is twenty seconds of outrageous courage. That's what is necessary to see your life and the lives around you radically changed by the right words at the right time. The dad came to a full stop and just stared. He could see her but she did not look up at him. He had a decision to make. He could keep walking past or he could step inside to introduce himself. So he took a deep breath and unexpectedly walked inside of the coffee shop. Then suddenly, he found himself just a few feet away from her. He could almost reach out and touch the table she was at…and he still had about ten seconds of courage left! So without hesitating further, he walked up to her and said something like, "Why would a beautiful woman like you ever talk to a guy like me." "Why not," she replied. And that – the dad told both his kids – is when the two of them became a possibility!

Twenty seconds of courage is all it takes to begin some startling conversations that forge new ground in our lives. "I'm sorry." "Please forgive me." "Will you marry me?" "May I share where I find

YOUNG LEADER SPOTLIGHT: A STORY OF TRANSFORMATION

Andrue ("Drue") Didyavong is an Asian-Pacific Islander young person who lives in the inner-city community of southeast San Diego. He attended Morse High School, played football, and participated in UYC's ministry for three years. Drue's father went to prison before he was born and has been there all his life. Yet Drue could see his heavenly father pursuing him.

Drue got a scholarship to attend FCA camp at UCLA for two summers. He subsequently completed two rigorous seasons of after-camp discipleship and became a leader at his school's outreach Bible club. "It was one of the best experiences of my life," he recalls, "teaching me that school and God can be intertwined."

Now a sophomore at SDSU, he has joined our team of adult leaders to take his friends through the same discipleship lessons he completed. The curriculum covers creation through urban apologetics from a Biblical perspective. Drue has multiplied himself and he can see his friends changing in the process!

As a young entrepreneur, Drue launched a Christian apparel company called AG2G (All Glory to God). Thanks to his vision, teenagers in southeast San Diego's schools are wearing clothing that represents Christ instead of a gang affiliation.

On top of all that, Drue recently joined UYC's comprehensive nine-month internship program for college students interested in developing their ministry gifts. His long-term goals are to become a Christian businessman and plant a church in the neighborhood where he lives!

hope in desperate times?" "Could we pray together?" "I love you." "I'm glad you were born." "What dreams can we chase together?" "Stop bullying her, she's my friend!" "May I share how Jesus has transformed my life?" "You're really good at science." "Thanks for being such a great friend." "I am blessed to have a dad like you." "You are the first person who really cared enough to listen." "I am amazed at how well you serve others." "You are smart." "Good job, son!" "I'm proud of you." "That's unjust and unfair to say about another person." "You're beautiful, honey." "Life's far better with you." "May I have this dance?" None of these statements take longer than a few seconds, but they can literally transform people's lives for decades, and for an eternity, to come.

The Dangers of Growing Up

One day while he was teaching, Jesus called a little child forward and had him stand in front of the disciples. "Unless you change," he said to the grown-ups, "and become like a little child, you will not enter the kingdom of God."[47] On another occasion, the disciples tried to block parents from bringing little children to Jesus. But Jesus became furious and said, "Let the little children come to me and do not hinder them. For the kingdom of God belongs to such as these."[48] When his disciples thought that Jesus was only interested in grown-ups, Jesus taught them that only those who approach God with the posture and attitude of a child can enter the kingdom of God. Then he took the children in his arms, laid his hands on them, and blessed them. Child-like faith approaches God with total abandon, dependence, boundless joy, and humility. Self-reliance and risk aversion are marks of grown-up calculations, but not of God's kingdom.

According to Jesus, the goal of the Christian life is not to grow old but to be born again. The call of discipleship is a call to change and become ever more child-like, not an excuse to stay child*ish*. Keeping our faith child-like takes hard work and discipline. It is far easier to grow up, forget how to dream, shackle our imaginations with grown-up practicalities and settle for a life that's safe, rational, and predictable. If we approach Jesus like grown-ups, we rely on our own strength, miss the kingdom, and get it wrong. Young people mentor me by teaching me how to humbly follow Jesus with passion, creativity, total dependence, and absolute trust. They can be role models who help me avoid the danger of growing up in the wrong ways, becoming too practical, too safe, and abandoning child-like faith. Our faith matures as we learn to dive more freely into the lap of our heavenly "Abba" Father with the gusto and glee of a little child.

My five-year-old daughter, Allegra, still runs to meet me whenever I come home. It's the best part of my day! With her arms outstretched, a huge silly grin on her face, and her bright blonde curly hair bobbing up and down, she screams, "Daddy!" She loves to play a game where I throw her up in the air and catch her. Each time she squeals with delight. Then she giggles and yells, "Again!" So I throw her up and catch her. And each time she hits my hands she immediately repeats, "Again daddy!" I toss her until my arms and shoulders burn. During these sacred moments, we both revel in the joy of her complete trust in her dad's ability to catch her every time. With her whole life literally in my hands, total trust becomes fun for children. She cannot get enough of it! If I ever dropped her, it would be over for Allegra. But that does not cross her mind because she is enthralled with the game we get to play over and over. It makes for an intimate portrait of child-like faith. If we fail to change and come to God like little children, we will miss the trust, abandonment, and thrill waiting for us in God's kingdom.

Child-like faith is different from grown-up faith. How many times have you and I heard a congregation full of adults joyfully yell, "Do it again!" right after the preacher finishes the Sunday sermon? When was the last time you heard grown-up people shout, "One more!" as soon as the offering plate is finished circulating? But that is exactly what child-like faith looks like if you ask Jesus. We can never get enough of our heavenly father and revel in spending time with him. Grown up faith keeps us checking our watches. Child-like faith keeps our eyes joyfully glued on Jesus. Because we trust him so much, we yell out in delight as he throws us into places where only he is able to catch us. Raw trust like this turns faith into an adventure and keeps our love relationship with Jesus alive and thriving.

Project 25 – Practicing Child Like Faith on a Citywide Scale

Not only does God want us to practice trusting him like a child, but he also wants us to learn to dream with him like little children. God-sized dreams are never just for us. They always have others front and center. Nine years ago, a youth pastor friend and I started a community service campaign because we wanted to inspire middle and high school students to attempt great things for

God.[49] We called it "Project 25," after the Parable of the Talents that Jesus told in Matthew 25. Each spring, we pass out $100 mini-grants to fifty Christian clubs that meet at public school campuses. Each group commits to read the parable, pray together, and then identify a practical need they want to meet in their school, community, city, state, or world. We do not want the money back. All we want is a 90-second YouTube video that tells the story of what they did with the funds. At the end of the semester, we host a worship night and red carpet awards program to honor students by presenting trophies to the first-, second-, and third-place teams who did the most incredible projects. I have been stunned by the creativity and the ingenuity displayed by San Diego's young people. Together they have partnered with groups to fund cancer treatments, develop peacemaking awards in the wake of gang violence, beautify beaches, combat human trafficking, free slaves in Sudan, drill fresh water wells in developing nations, feed the homeless, share audio Bibles with pre-literate societies, support refugees, and spread the love of Jesus in countless ways. Over the past nine years, a total of 170,000 hours of volunteer service have been performed by San Diego's young people invested into projects that touch local and global causes. To recognize the achievements of students, mayor Kevin Faulconer issued a Proclamation declaring May 11, 2018 to be "Project 25 Day" in the City of San Diego. One year a group of twenty-five schools in New York City joined the challenge. We were thrilled to have five new campuses in Mexico participating in 2018, along with a school in Atlanta!

Learning to Dream Again

Several years ago, we brought a motivational school assembly program to a very affluent private school in San Diego's North County.

Since starting UYC, I have watched this same assembly team make over a hundred presentations at diverse schools throughout San Diego County over the past nine years. We took them all over the map, to inner-city schools, suburban schools, middle school campuses, high school campuses, and even a vocational training center. But this group of students stood out like no other. During the course of the assembly, the presenters ask the audience to voluntarily share one dream that they have for their lives. This was the only assembly ever when we heard nothing but cold, stony silence. Everyone was more concerned about what others thought of them than with the dream God planted in their hearts. They kept looking left and right at their friends instead of courageously speaking up about a dream God had given them. Immediately after the high school presentation, four hundred middle school students attended the same program. It was striking how much of a difference a few grade levels could make. The younger middle school kids were quick to jump up, participate, and unashamed to share their dreams in public. In only a few years they would turn into high school students with an increased risk of becoming pre-grown-ups who forget how to dream.

In order to overcome this common danger, Joseph developed the discipline of remembering the dreams God gave to him as a teenager (Genesis 42:9). For those who know the story, Joseph's dreams began at age seventeen, but they did not start becoming visible until he hit thirty. That is when he moved from prison to the palace. It was not until he was thirty-nine that his family returned and bowed down to him as his original two dreams depicted. What a long journey of faithfulness! He had to endure painful opposition, abandonment, and false accusations. He probably wondered if he had heard from God correctly or if he just imagined that his life would serve some higher purpose. In fact, he had many opportunities to give up. He was betrayed by his family, sold as a slave, relentlessly hit on by his boss's wife, framed for a crime he did not commit, and forgotten to rot in jail. Yet he rose to the top of whatever situation he found himself in. He was the favorite of his father's house, ran the slave quarters for Potipher, became head of the prison second only to the warden, and then eventually head of Egypt, answering only to Pharaoh himself.

Joseph's dreams proved bigger than something just for him. God literally used the dreams of a faithful teenager to save the nations of Israel and Egypt (and other surrounding countries) from famine and extinction. When I talk to young people about living out their God-given dreams, I tell them that finding out their personal mission is a matter of life and death for others. The dreams God gives us are intended for more than our stories or families alone. As Joseph said when summarizing his life story to his brothers, "You intended to harm me, but God intended it all for good. He brought me to this position so I could save the lives of many people."[50] The entire story of God's people would have ended tragically if Joseph had given up on his God-given dreams. The nation of Israel may have died of famine had Joseph abandoned his dreams.

When I got ordained for full-time ministry in 2008, one of my dear friends from the black Pentecostal tradition came and closed out my ordination service with a charge. It is the same challenge I want to share with you as this chapter draws to a close. Citing one of his heroes, Miles Monroe, my friend told me, and those assembled, that the most valuable land on planet Earth is not the oil fields in the Middle East, it is not the diamond mines in South Africa, nor is it a gated community in La Jolla or Rancho Santa Fe, California. The most valuable land on planet Earth, he assured us, is the cemeteries. Cemeteries are where all the dreams that

YOUNG LEADER SPOTLIGHT: A STORY OF TRANSFORMATION

As a senior running back for the Morse High School Tigers, Martell Irby led a weekly outreach Bible club on campus at SCPA High School in San Diego's inner-city.

As a proven leader on and off the field, Martell took responsibility for teaching his younger teammates using discipleship lessons that he completed over the previous two summers.

Martell also came up with the idea to gather at midfield for a public, student-led prayer with his team and their opponents after every game throughout the season. Since his prayers are student initiated and student led, they cannot be stopped by anyone.

The above photo was taken after a particularly contentious game against Mount Miguel High School. The opposing team committed two flagrant face mask penalties, broke another athlete's femur, and a fight erupted in the stands. Nonetheless, Martell had the maturity and composure to bring both teams together for a closing prayer focused on Jesus.

never made it out of people lay undeveloped and trapped for all eternity. There is a cure for cancer, he declared, locked away in a cemetery because a brilliant junior high boy gave up his dream of becoming a scientist because his friends made fun of him for being smart. There is a cure for poverty, he said, sealed away forever in a tomb because someone let the pressures and practicalities of life consume their attention and their dream of a better tomorrow slipped silently away. There is a plan for overcoming America's racial divisions trapped somewhere in a grave because a young dreamer stayed silent and did not dare to speak out about a bigger vision for a reconciled society. There is a vision for ending domestic violence and depression forever lost because it never got out of the soul who carried it. Somewhere in a cemetery, there is a movement whereby millions will be introduced to Jesus as LORD and Savior, but it never got written down to get outside the body of the dreamer. "So when you're done with your ministry, Nate," he told me, "make sure that you die empty."[51]

Whatever God has put in you, get it out. Develop it. Nurture it. The world needs it. Put it to work! And be sure to die empty. May the young people – and the young at heart – in our cities not let anyone look down on them – not by the church, or the government, or any institution, or any family members, or friends, or themselves – but may they set the example for other believers in faith, in love, and in purity. My dream is that my life will inspire all the young people and emerging leaders I touch to die empty too. Whatever God has put inside me was intended to get out for the world around me. That is how I want every teenager I encounter to live their life too.

five

SHALOM: WHOLE PEOPLE AND WHOLE COMMUNITIES

My wife is half Italian. One of our favorite places to go out to eat is Little Italy, a quaint section of downtown San Diego near the waterfront. A few of the streets feel like a couple blocks of Florence got magically transported to Southern California. For me, the fettuccine, tortellini, chianti, cappuccino, and gelato all combine for an exquisite evening. Experiencing the smells, tastes, people, music, lights, and architecture of Little Italy makes me hungry for the real thing. After leaving there, I cannot wait to experience the homeland. As a foretaste, *Little* Italy makes me yearn to visit *Big* Italy again! That is exactly how God calls Christians to inhabit and work in this world where we find ourselves. As believers, we are charged to make the neighborhoods we live in – and the relationships that grow there – more representative of our true home in heaven. As citizens of God's kingdom, all of us are ultimately foreigners setting up lives here while in exile. Whether we realize it or not, every time we pray the LORD's prayer, we are asking God to intervene on earth by bringing his holiness, kingdom agenda, daily bread, forgiveness, and reconciliation in ways that reflect our true identify and eternal homeland. As we pursue God's will on earth *just as* as it is in heaven, our job is to make others hungry to visit and experience our family's original country. Our lives and communities should serve as a preview of God's coming kingdom. Already, but not yet. We inhabit and embody the tension of living fully "in the world but not of the world."[52]

Citizens of a Kingdom Worth Living In

As God's people, we are looking forward to – and are part of – a future/present city worth living in forever. Gold, the Bible tells us, is so plentiful there that it will be the concrete of this new metropolis. San Diego Gas and Electric (SDG&E), my hometown utility provider, will not be necessary because the light of God will fill the city day and night. Police will be out of jobs because there will be no more crime. Kleenex will go out of business because there will be no more tears. Doctors will be looking for transferable job skills because there will be no such thing as sickness or disease. Counselors will find no clients because broken relationships and depression will be history. Morticians will have plentiful vacation time. No one will be interested in numbing their awareness through narcotics as many do on Earth. People living in this new eternal country will enjoy taking in the fully perfect reality that surrounds them. This kingdom we belong to is a beautiful place. As Christ's ambassadors, we get to see approximations of it invade our present in concrete time and space. It is so captivating we cannot help but invite others into it. All the while, we allow its values to break into the present moment to transform contemporary realities.

While I was speaking to a group of junior high students in the affluent community of Coronado, an eighth-grade boy in the back confidently told me his life was going just fine without Jesus. He was well dressed, popular, and had all his material needs met. To engage him, I asked if the life he had now was so good that he would want it to continue on forever. To my surprise, he quipped, "No, not at all. But it will be fine for about seventy years or so." I then went on to propose that life to the fullest with Christ is *so* good that it can be enjoyed forever and ever. That's why God designed eternity for us and placed it in our hearts. He wants us to enjoy him forever. The indescribable majesty and wonder of God make it possible for us to discover exciting new things about him every day for all eternity. It will never get boring!

My Master of Divinity degree is from Gordon-Conwell Theological Seminary (GCTS), an interdenominational evangelical divinity school in suburban Boston. My Ph.D. in Religion came from Claremont Graduate University, a pluralistic – and in some aspects agnostic – school of religion just outside of Los Angeles. The former academic institution primarily emphasizes the importance of spiritual salvation for the individuals in the next life.[53] The latter favored reforming social systems and fighting macro injustices in the present world. Intriguingly, each group got part of the puzzle right. When I read the scriptures, I hear God's word calling both individuals and social structures to repentance, renewal, and regeneration through Christ in a way that harmonizes with God's kingdom reign, on earth as it is in heaven. Broken systems and broken people need to heal and become whole again. Broken systems create more broken people. Broken people shape, and preside over, broken systems and make matters worse. Macro forces accelerate individual problems and vice versa. This dynamic interplay captures the way social actors create, and are acted upon by, the structures they inhabit. Conservatives correctly point out that all individuals are sinners in need of personal grace and forgiveness. Liberals tend to focus less on interpersonal "sins" and failings while pointing out how the poor, weak, and vulnerable often are sinned *against* by bigger systems of society. Preserving both aspects of "salvation" – understanding that individuals and systems can be transformed – are important if we are going to have a fully biblical picture of God's work in the world.

A Just Peace Is More Than "Just Peace"

The Hebrew word "shalom" is often translated in English as "peace" and usually defined as the absence of hostility. While this rendering is not itself inaccurate, the beautiful Hebrew concept of shalom captures a fuller sense of social flourishing, fullness of life, balanced justice, and thriving for all peoples in a shared community. It implies that both individual and societal transformation is taking place. The shalom of God's kingdom has the power to bring hope from the future into present realities and historical circumstances. Under the rubric of shalom, one realizes that spiritual and material concerns are not always separate realities but can be interconnected and interwoven. From this perspective, we can ask what it looks like for a neighborhood or school system to flourish. Could an educational system be reborn? Can a whole church get "saved" by engaging its neighborhood? By dreaming together about a shared tomorrow, could it be possible for believers to be part of a "foretaste" of God's kingdom "here on earth as it is in heaven?" I believe the answer is "Yes!"

Public school ministry presents the ideal place for personal evangelism and social engagement to go hand in hand. When done properly, caring for the body (through a church providing a fresh grocery program), the mind (through tutoring), and the spirit (student-led evangelism/discipleship) can go toward making a young person whole. Once a student begins moving toward wholeness, however, it is important for them to have opportunities to participate in a society that is not coming apart at the seams. Shalom, therefore, proclaims that practical job skills and educational resources matter to urban young people *along with* a personal relationship with Jesus Christ as LORD and savior.

As a lifelong student of ethics, people sometimes ask me which I support more, the right wing or the left? My response is that the church needs *both* wings to get the plane off the ground! I want young people I work with to know about the book of *Job* in the Bible while *also* being able to retain a viable *job* after the Bible study is over. Both are vitally important. Instead of thinking in either/or dichotomies when it comes to individual or social transformation, God's kingdom shalom prophetically calls for a more robust and complete vision of social reality.

The wholeness of God's shalom brings together concepts that were never intended to be divided or divorced. It cohesively reunites and balances the individual with the social, the physical with the spiritual, this world with the next life, and immanence with transcendence. Through a practical and concretized theology of shalom, we can work to develop approximations, foretastes, and glimpses of the kingdom of God. The younger, upcoming generation is hungry to see American Christianity address them and demonstrate how the gospel applies to their demographic as public school students. After all, the majority of America's teenagers attend public schools. As believers, we must be able to show that Jesus has relevance to their life situation and the issues that they face.

The great abolitionist preacher and evangelist, Charles Finney, is a historical example of shalom taking concrete form. Finney

Ordinary classrooms become holy ground when student leaders step up to share Jesus with their friends at public schools.

Motivational school assemblies connect with the entire student body while providing a moral compass for young people.

Student leader training equips and inspires the next generation to dream with God about His will for their friends at school.

UYC's Late Lunch Learning Lab brings local congregations together to share best practices for effective campus ministry.

We end each summer with a back-to-school BBQ where students graduate from an intensive discipleship initiative.

Students at Lincoln High School form a giant prayer circle in response to an altercation between campus police and students.

Dàn Bauch engages with students during a middle school assembly where participates push through life's obstacles.

Jason Crawley "speaks life" to students during one of five consecutive assemblies at a San Diego high school.

At the conclusion of the summer discipleship program, students choose to be baptized as a public profession of faith in Christ.

Our partnership with FCA allows us to bring 150 kids from San Diego to UCLA for a Christ-centered sports camp every summer.

New student-led faith clubs are sprouting up at public schools all over San Diego County...
100 and counting!

Volunteers enjoy a school beautification and mural project at a National City school.
Photo Credit: Concrete and Canvas.

Young leaders and their mentors celebrate graduation from our summer discipleship experience.

Our partnership with Metamorfosis in Mexico allows us to care for students on both sides of the border.

My incredible wife, Angela (right) always jumps wholeheartedly into whatever God calls us to do. Here she is with Karla, an amazing student who earned a study Bible by completing our summer discipleship program.

Up close with some of the students following a day of assemblies and workshops in Tijuana, Mexico.

Jesse Matone, one of our faithful apprentices, gains valuable experience by serving as a guest speaker at local high school clubs.

When I see prayer circles like this forming in our city, I know the future is in good hands. These kids give me hope!

My oldest son, Russell (holding the football), has grown up with some good high school role models who stick close to Jesus.

Ministry in southeast San Diego would not happen without Dalvon Logan (left) and Martel Irby (right). This dynamic duo loves countless students in the name of Jesus. As a student leader, Martel takes his friends through the same Bible lessons he studied.

My good friend Steve Barclay coordinates school beautification projects at Hoover High School every year.

Campus clubs thrive in all shapes and sizes when they have support from faithful congregations like The Grove Church.

Before the district illegally banned it in 2015, this student faith club at Point Loma High School grew to one of the largest in the city. Happily, they have been reinstated and are growing again.

Project 25 draws nearly 1,200 students from San Diego and Mexico. They come to celebrate their Christ-centered service projects that show others what's possible when young people join together and serve Jesus wholeheartedly.

We believe the best is yet to come in the US and Mexico as young people seek first God's kingdom and its righteousness.

Crawford High School won the "Mob Award" at Project 25 for bringing the largest group.

Congratulations to San Diego High School, Fallbrook High School, and CYCTE Primo Tapia on their three-way tie for first place in the 2018 Project 25 community service challenge. Altogether, students generated 59,595 hours of volunteer service during the past school year.

commonly asked listeners to make a personal decision to follow Jesus and then simultaneously implored them to join the anti-slavery movement of his day. Personal faith in Christ carried with it profound social consequences. Finney saw no division between promoting individual piety while also calling listeners to engage the social structures that do not meet the standards of God's justice. Finney did not conceive of someone being "at peace" with God until just social structures made it possible for his audience to be "at a just-peace" with fellow humans present in the nation and beyond. In his *Original Memoirs*, Finney writes:

> This was what we aimed to accomplish, to preach the Gospel, especially to the poor. When I first went to New York, I had made up my mind on the subject of the slavery question and was exceedingly anxious to arouse public attention to the subject. I did not, however, turn aside to make it a hobby, or divert attention of the people from the work of converting souls. Nevertheless, in my prayers and preaching I so often alluded to slavery and denouncing it, that a considerable excitement came to exist among the people.[54]

Shalom's "job," then, in any era, becomes that of bringing about concrete change and action within society wherever current conditions do not line up with the "just-peace" that God's kingdom requires. Just as nineteenth-century converts to Christianity were challenged to take on the social evil of slavery as a direct outworking of their newfound faith within Finney's ministry, could it be that a new social movement could arise at the intersection of Christians and American education where believers see public school engagement as a vital expression of genuine Christian faith? How else can we reach out to the coming generations to see them thrive in every way? Withdrawing into an enclave of safe private schools, isolated congregations, and home school environments cannot be the only response if we endeavor to help God's kingdom reign extend to the next generation.

As with Charles Finney, many revivals in US history were attached to social movements. I dream of a movement where churches embrace public schools, education, and students as a vital part of their kingdom mission. Then we can begin to see vital and needed changes sweep across our country. In my city and county of San Diego, for example, one out of every five high school students will not graduate.[55] Among certain statewide populations in California, the dropout rate is as high as one in three.[56] Gang violence, broken families, hunger, and hopelessness threaten the dreams and vitality of many vibrant young lives. As mentioned before, many of San Diego's most impoverished secondary schools are named after US Presidents: Hoover High School, Lincoln High School, Roosevelt Middle School, and Wilson Middle School. Yet far too many of our city's students are missing out on the elusive "American dream." Educational researcher Jonathan Kozol calls such disparities between rich and poor children in the US public school system *Savage Inequalities.*[57] Despite such urgent social realities, many Christian congregations from across the theological spectrum have managed to isolate themselves from engagement with the next generation and function independently away from the pressing needs of the hungry, the sick, and the marginalized. Happily, more and more churches in our city are dreaming bigger about life's possibilities for young people in San Diego. Will you dream and live it out with us? I hope so. In writing these pages, I invite you to let God break your heart by what is happening to his kids. He wants them back. And he wants fullness of life for them – both now and forever – back on the priority list for his followers.

As Jesus said, "the harvest is plentiful but the workers are few."[58] He did not say "the synagogue or church attendees are few." He says the true workers are few. That is who he is looking for, people who will join him in bringing the whole gospel to the whole world.[59] Jesus then asks us to pray to the LORD of the harvest so more people will be sent out to roll up their sleeves and get dirty for the sake of the lost and oppressed.

Churches that engage schools get firsthand opportunities to shape the individuals and the structures that mold students' hearts and minds. In the gospels, Jesus describes his followers as salt and light. If all the salt and light flees from public schools because we are unhappy with the sex education curriculum or theories of Darwinism, then should we be surprised if our nation's public schools experience further decay or growing darkness? Salt and light both have a transforming effect on whatever they touch. Once making contact, salt and light always wins. When we put salt on meat – I heard one preacher say – the meat always gets saltier, the salt never gets meatier."[60] When I turn a light on in my bathroom to shave early in the morning, the light always chases the darkness away. The darkness never implodes into the light bulb and destroys it. That only happens in *Harry Potter* movies! Since salt and light has properties that give it power over decay and darkness, believers can stay in – or at least engage with – public schools with boldness and confidence knowing that Christ in them is greater than the cultural forces that surround them.

Salt and light, however, never functions alone. Salt always travels together with other crystals and photons always travel in waves. A single light particle or solo salt crystal may not make much of an impact when trying to bring change on its own. In fact, it might just get consumed by the decay and darkness that surrounds it. This is why God's word tells us not to "forsake meeting together with other believers as some are in the habit of doing."[61] By working together in groups, light rays and pieces of salt can transform the surroundings that they are poured out onto. This is why I am such a big proponent of student-led faith clubs at public schools. This is also why I am such a big advocate of churches and ministries working *together* to provide support and care for kids. As a team, young people can stand up and make a tangible difference in the places God has planted them. Together, churches, parents, youth ministry organizations, and community groups can unite to support and empower young people to achieve their God-given dreams. Every Shadrach needs a Meshach and an Abednego. Every Shaunae needs a Michelle and an Alicia. Every Sabastian, needs a Mateo and an Alejandro.

Where I come from on the east coast, salt is poured out on ice to keep people from slipping. Similarly, God pours out his people all over our society to prevent moral falls and failures within a culture headed down a slippery slope with zero traction. But salt can only bring transformation when it *touches* something. It has to make contact and be pressed into the culture. Even if it gets stepped on and ground down, it is still accomplishing its mission as it becomes part of the ice and transforms it. Society's pathways of life are safer to walk on, and less slippery, with genuine Christians around. Imagine city streets after a bad snow storm. If there was no such thing as salt, a neighborhood would be at a standstill. Similarly, the power of the Holy Spirit moves through God's people to bring needed motion and change in each environment where Jesus' ambassadors have been strategically placed.

Salt and light must often be absorbed into the substance it hopes to transform. This is the power of incarnational ministry. "Drive-by disciples" will not be effective at bringing neighborhood change like those who enter in and become a true part of a community's fabric. Often times, salt (and light to a certain extent) must be poured out – or shine out – to the point of no return in order to transform its surroundings. Salt crystals do not get to go back home to the shaker after the job is done. They are committed to the task for good. Light shines brightly, but the same photon never returns to the bulb or star from which it first came. Sacrifice is a crucial ingredient that leads to community sanctification. Commitment and consecration must be part of the package if we want to see lasting transformation in the people, families, and neighborhoods we love most. Jesus said that there is no greater love than when someone willingly lays down his life for a friend.[62]

By counting the cost of discipleship, God's people – acting as salt and light – can change the environment around them in ways that transform both individuals and society as a whole. When both people and systems are called to repent and follow Jesus, this shift announces God's kingdom reign "on earth as it is in heaven." The power of the LORD's prayer, though, comes when prayed corporately and lived out in groups. The plural pronouns in this well-worn petition instructed ancient – and now modern – disciples to seek God's kingdom together as a collective call and response. For God's name to be holy, God's kingdom to come, and God's will to be done, for daily bread and forgiveness to flow freely, asking and obeying have to take place in community. We petition as a group and obey as a family. Then we can experience the benefits both individually and corporately.

The dream of shalom for America's cities, its young people, and institutions cannot be achieved in isolation. Salt crystals and light photons must engage together, as designed, in order for their life-giving and healing properties to take effect. Whole people and whole communities – the individual and the social group – go hand in hand. Through a dynamic interplay, they shape and remake each other. By taking residence in single persons and shared communities, shalom spreads throughout the schools, neighborhoods, churches, cities, families, and young people of our nation. It overwhelms despair, brokenness, death, lies, emptiness, and chaos. It marks a new beginning for young people, the hopeful dawn of a kingdom worth living in, led by a leader worth following. As we learn to pray the LORD's prayer and act together, we often discover that God uses us to become the answers to some of those same prayers.

six

KINGDOM COLLABORATION: WORKING AND SWIMMING TOGETHER AS ONE

When Jesus calls Peter to be his disciple through a miraculous catch of fish, he forever alters the life of an unsuspecting Galilean tradesman. Jesus repurposes Peter's fishing gift by teaching him to go after something that lasts forever: other men and women made in God's image. A key part of the lesson for Peter that day is relevant for contemporary ministers too. *Following Jesus means learning to be humble enough to call out and ask partners for help.* This is how Luke describes what happened after Peter threw his empty net back into the water one more time:

> And when they had done this, they enclosed a large number of fish, and their nets were breaking. They signaled to their partners in the other boat to come and help them. And they came and filled both the boats, so that they began to sink. But when Simon Peter saw it, he fell down at Jesus' knees, saying, "Depart from me, for I am a sinful man, O Lord." For he and

all who were with him were astonished at the catch of fish they had taken, and so were James and John, sons of Zebedee, who were partners with Simon.[63]

Through this story, Peter helps us all admit that Jesus gives us God-sized tasks too big and important to accomplish alone. During his first day of on-the-job-training, Peter saw that his net was starting to break on its own due to the load. If he did not quickly learn to work together with others, valuable fish – which clearly represent the souls of people here – would be lost for good.[64] Even after his partners joined in, there were so many fish that *both* boats began to sink.[65]

There are no accidents in Jesus' words or actions in this story. It is fascinating that he forces Peter to partner together with other disciples during their first face-to-face encounter. Unity, humility, and interdependence represent some of the crucial kingdom lessons Jesus experientially taught his new disciples from the very beginning. Immediately, Peter drops to his knees and cries out, "Depart from me, for I am a sinful man, O Lord."[66] Peter had to repent for being small minded and dreaming of a life tiny enough for him to control and accomplish alone. Through an unexpected spark from Christ's supernatural power, Peter could feel the "weight of glory" taking the form of freshly-caught fish flapping around his old boat.[67] He knew he must let Jesus revolutionize the way he thought about his life, his ministry, and his future. Do you dare to let Jesus climb into your ministry and life to do the same? Souls and a kingdom witness for your city may hinge on your answer.

The scriptures tell us that Peter and his partners were "astonished" by the catch of fish that they had taken that day. If we are not currently "astonished" by what God is doing in our churches, youth ministries, or communities, perhaps it is time to drop to our knees and confess our sins of isolation and prideful illusions of independence. Then we must ask Jesus to give us a new vision and mindset – one so large that it requires kingdom partners to succeed. "Do not be afraid," Jesus assures his brand new kingdom recruits, "from now on you will be catching people."[68] In this passage of scripture, it is no surprise that John goes out of his way to mention twice that Peter's partners – James and John – were likewise *astonished* at what Jesus did through them as they worked together. *Truly astonishing ministry begins to happen when disciples partner together in God's kingdom work!* That is exactly what I want to unpack and convince you of through this chapter.

No one church, ministry, or organization can get close to meeting all the needs, or actualizing all the potential, at a school or in a neighborhood alone. *When we settle for independence, we settle for less for us and the people Jesus calls us to reach.* This includes mega churches that – like the sun in a solar system – produce lots of beautiful bright light, heat, energy, and life. Yet sometimes their gravitational pull is so strong that their people have trouble escaping the draw to interact with other smaller – and equally vital – planets in the neighboring "solar system." Big churches need little churches. Little churches need big churches. Medium-sized congregations can be mighty when they band together. We will never make the most of all the opportunities in front of us on our own. Therefore, we need each other and a new spirit of interdependence between youth organizations, churches, and schools in our cities. Suspicion and distrust abound for those who think they are the only player in town that does the *really* good work or that *truly* understands the *best* way to reach people. Often, as Jesus' modern disciples, we operate out of fear that someone else will steal our "secret sauce" recipe for ministry success if they get too close. Asking, learning, and celebrating the successes of others are the antidotes to pride.

Walking by faith, sharing credit, and trusting God's work enough to journey together are the antidotes to fear.

We must be willing to share ideas, resources, people, cash, and results in order to see the kingdom of God manifested in the lives of America's youth. Leaders must learn to lay down their egos and logos for the sake of something better: the well-being and eternal destiny of young people in their community. Some Christian leaders, for example, have a "sum zero" idea when it comes to ministry funding. They shy away from collaborating because they are concerned that someone else may steal their slice of the ministry pie. Similarly, churches are afraid to work together because they fear another pastor will commandeer their people or their best, new, creative ministry ideas. This type of win/lose thinking assumes that if one ministry gets something good, then it automatically means that someone else misses out. Shifting our perspective to kingdom thinking, where all churches exist as agents who serve the broader kingdom of God, can revolutionize ministry. In my experience, I have seen the pie grow when the right partners get together. The slices actually get bigger for everyone and there are more of them to go around. This shifts our thinking from scarcity to abundance.

Another important part of Jesus' on-the-job training with Peter came during the second miraculous catch of fish at the end of John's gospel. Jesus kept returning to this theme in a way that met Peter on his own turf and spoke to him in terms he could easily relate to. On many of these occasions, Jesus chose to walk alongside and live out this story with Peter personally. At this stage of the narrative, we rejoin Peter after he has denied Christ three times prior to the crucifixion. Shame and uncertainty drove him back to his previous occupation of fishing for ordinary fish that do not last forever. This was familiar and comfortable territory for Peter, an easy place for the future rock of the church and Pentecost's soon-to-be evangelistic preacher to hide. The risen Christ had to meet him back at the waters, remind him how it all began, forgive him, and reinstate him to full-time ministry. There is something unique about this second "prophetic" catch of fish, though, that makes it more than just a reminder of the first call. Jesus miraculously empowers Peter to haul in a peculiar catch of fish that contains a spectacular lesson for disciples of every era. John records it this way in Chapter 21 of his gospel:

> When they got out on land, they saw a charcoal fire in place, with fish laid out on it, and bread. Jesus said to them, 'Bring some of the fish that you have just caught.' So Simon went aboard and hauled the net ashore, full of large fish, 153 of them. And although there were so many, the net was not torn.[69]

Why is God so specific in this passage about the number of fish Peter caught that day? While impressive, 153 does not appear to be nearly as many fish as the first miraculous catch that almost sunk two boats. Nor does it rival the large amount of bread and fish Jesus multiplied to feed thousands upon thousands in the wilderness on several occasions. Our LORD is easily capable of bringing in more, so why does he make a special point for the disciples – past and present – with the math wrapped up in this fishing expedition? Surely it is meant to provide more than just eye-witness specificity. Jesus wants modern disciples like us to catch the lesson too.

Interestingly enough, Saint Jerome writes that Greek zoologists of his day believed there were 153 different species of fish present in the Mediterranean region.[70] Could Jesus have supernaturally allowed Peter to catch fish representing many of these different species in his net that day?[71] Saint Augustine, similarly, points

out that 153 is a significant number due to its "triangular" quality, representing the sum total of the first seventeen integers added
together.[72] In other words, Augustine saw this number as a sym-
bolic all-inclusive sign. The church will be made up of all figures
and measures added together to form one new community. Both
saints – along with many commentators – make the case that this
miracle prophetically signifies the "universality" and broad draw of
the global church Jesus wants to plant through Peter. Could it be
that Jesus, by reinstating Peter through a second miraculous catch
of fish, was also giving him a preview of the diversity of people
and cultures who are unexpectedly bound up together as members of God's kingdom family? As part of the eclectic people of
God surprisingly caught up by an external and eternal actor bigger
than ourselves, we should plan on working with – and going after
– every type of person. Jesus could have miraculously placed a
representative of many species of fish in that net to get us ready for
similar representation from all stripes and style of humanity within
our communities of faith. Unlike the first miraculous catch of fish
that Peter experienced, the second time around we read that the
net did *not* start to break. Therefore, we can conclude that God's
kingdom "net" is big enough and strong enough to hold all different shapes, sizes, colors, and personalities in the sea of humanity
without breaking either.

When we do notice divisions between God's people, we are
not witnessing the cords of God's strength breaking or his passion
for unity fraying apart. Instead, it might just be that people keep
trying to jump out of the boat after the catch because they prefer
to swim with their own kind and in schools of their own choosing.
Jesus' miraculous work in our lives creates a "new school" made
up of *every* tongue and tribe and nation. That is what Jesus' kingdom is all about. At the seminary where I am writing, a fortuitous

picture hangs on the wall depicting this second miraculous catch of fish. "The Great Catch" (1993) by John August Swanson beautifully captures the astonishing unity and wonder of this miracle moment.[73] What I love about it is all the bright and distinctly different colors and sizes of fish that the disciples are pulling in as they work together. The fish did not choose to be caught any more than they chose *who* else they got caught up with.

As God's people, similarly captured by his grace, we do not get to object if different species of fish get rescued along with us. The diverse fish, surprised to find themselves in Peter's net that day, did not have a say in the matter. Neither do we. Through God's action and not our own volition, we unavoidably become part of God's kingdom when we are first caught. This automatically places us on a team, in a family, and within a movement that is larger than us and more diverse than we could ever imagine. This was a preview of – and precedent for – the beautiful variety, creativity, and diversity Christ initiates when placing us in his new church. When we see unity like that – with every possible species and color swimming in one net – it is *simply astonishing* for us and others to behold! It is not natural, only supernatural. It can only happen when God performs a miracle meant to arrest our attention and interrupt our separate lives. Supernatural unity like that proves there is something otherworldly going on. Ordinarily, fish – just like humans – prefer to swim only with their "own kind." The miraculous part of this catch is that Jesus taught all the different species of fish to swim together.

Some well-known church growth experts actually advise congregations to keep people groups separate in order to make everyone more comfortable when they attend church.[74] Jesus shares a bolder and more miraculous vision (read: *astonishing*) with Peter during this field trip to the sea. Whether rich or poor, young or old, healthy or sick, no matter what color, in spite of past fail-ures, regardless of geographic longitude or latitude, no matter the intelligence, Jesus trained Peter to see infinite value in a beauti-fully diverse people group that only God could bring together. All shapes, sizes, colors, and swimming styles get caught up in the unbreakable net of grace that holds Christ's kingdom together. Later at Pentecost, this vision would start to become reality. Peter's sermon drew "devout men and women from every nation under heaven."[75] Countless language groups came together into the sin-gular net of God's kingdom as 3,000 people repented of their sins, got baptized, and joined the multi-ethnic church on the day it was born.[76] The waters of baptism publicly signify that we are washed anew, resurrected from death to life with Christ, and – not unlike fish – caught out of one reality to experientially enter an astonish-ing new community.

Defeating A Prowling Lion

Scripture teaches us that followers of Jesus face a real spiritual enemy. Know it or not, like it or not, believe it or not, we are liter-ally at war every day. Peter describes the devil as a constant hunter looking for his next vulnerable victim with these words, "Be alert and sober minded. Your enemy the devil prowls around like a roar-ing lion looking for someone to devour" (1 Peter 5:8). According to C.S. Lewis, the enemy of our soul gains power over us if we become unhealthily fascinated by demons or when we believe that they do not exist.[77] Therefore, we need to be aware of the strategies of this dangerous lion.

My middle son, Rocco, loves to watch the show *Africa's Deadliest Predators* with me. He's fascinated by studying lions as they stalk their prey. A prowling lioness is most effective when animals falls for her twin tactics of fear and isolation. If packs of wildebeest, water buffalo, or other horned meals in the safari remain vigilant and stand shoulder to shoulder, they cannot be caught. Lions stand down and call off pursuit when they notice unity in the herd that cannot be disrupted. Part of me wishes I could have a moment with the leaders at the wildebeest community forum to coach them up a bit. If given the opportunity, I would tell them to stand side by side and fearlessly lower their horns whenever the enemy approaches. Even a mighty pride of lions will back off when they see the herd coordinated and unified without wavering. Aside from ambush, the only tactic the prowling lion has is to divide the herd by trying to scare a few of them into running off alone. United we stand. Divided and alone we fall. The need for this simple but forgotten lesson gets repeated every time the devil devours another victim that decided to go solo. It is no accident that scripture equates the lethal strategies of the devil with that of a prowling lion. Whenever the enemy attacks, the antidote is unity and community! Spiritually speaking, the degree to which we are able to stand together as one is literally a matter of life and death.

Giving Away Life So It May Be Found

Life with Jesus in God's kingdom is counterintuitive. Jesus had some strong words for those of us who claim to be his followers. He turns our thinking – as we know it – upside down. In Luke 17:33 he challenges his audience by declaring, "Whoever works to preserve his life will lose it, but whoever loses his life will keep it." Those who try to hang on to their own lives, find them slipping through their fingers. I heard one pastor say it is like trying to grab large amounts of Jello with clinched fists. The tighter we squeeze, the quicker it gets away and disappears through our fingers. Those who serendipitously give away their lives for the kingdom and the gospel find life to the fullest.

I believe Jesus meant this principle to be true not only for individual people but also for organizations and churches on a corporate or citywide level too. If we try to save our church or organization more than the kingdom, we can end up losing it. When we give our ministry away for this gospel, however, we fortuitously discover that God provides the funding, statistics, staff, and results that we were hoping for when we contemplated doing it alone. In the end — as our friends at the National Network of Youth Ministries say so well — we are "better together" when it comes to advancing God's kingdom. Individual churches, denominations, or ministry organizations exist as agents tasked *primarily (first)* with advancing God's kingdom "on earth as it is in heaven," not seeking their own institutional survival.[78] If we seek God's kingdom first, all the other things follow after it. Jesus said it well. "Seek first the kingdom of God and its righteousness (read: *right relationships*) and all these other things will be added unto you as well."[79] Hence the Church (capital C) encompasses all local Christ-centered congregations, denominational bodies, and ministry organizations and exists primarily for the benefit of its non-members.[80] All throughout the country and planet, Christians ask for radical unity every time they recite God's heartbeat expressed in the LORD's prayer. Often we just do not realize what we are asking for! At times we rush through the phrase, "May your kingdom come and your will be done on earth as it is in heaven" while sitting in divided congregations without grasping the true implications of the words we pray together.[81]

We need to begin viewing the parts of Christ's body as more than different individuals within a solitary local congregation.

While this is certainly one true and vital aspect for our understanding, we must expand our view to see the different *organs* of Christ body made up of the various *organizations* within an entire city, community, or region. Together the collective strength and specialization of Christ's body can be appreciated and coordinated on a macro (citywide) level as well as a micro (congregational) level. Paul describes this reality to the Corinthians using these words:

> For just as the body is one and has many members, and all the members of the body, though many, are one body, it is with Christ. For in one Spirit we were all baptized into one body – Jews or Greeks, slaves or free – and all were made to drink of one Spirit. For the body does not consist of one member but of many.... The eye cannot say to the hand, "I have no need of you," nor again the head to the feet, "I have no need of you."

When we stand united as one body, we are able to defeat the strategies on the devil. When James tells us to stand firm, resist the devil, and he will flee from you, I can only assume that he means we must stand firm together as a unified herd.[82]

Spiritual Gang Bangers

Pastors who fall for the devil's tricks of fear and isolation run the risk of unwittingly behaving like "spiritual gang bangers" instead of kingdom saints.[83] We are all guilty of this at times. It is human nature to compete and protect our own turf. As we mature in Christ, however, we learn to catch ourselves more quickly when the Holy Spirit convicts us. If left unchecked, we begin going to war with ourselves and we forget who the true enemy is. When we tell kids in the inner-city not to gang-bang (participate in gang-related activities) by viewing the "other" through an "us" versus "them" lens on the streets, young people will call our bluff when they watch pastors do the same thing inside church sanctuaries. While telling young people to avoid the battle of the Bloods versus Crips, religious leaders zealously reinforce the divide between the Baptists and Calvinists. When protecting turf, reputation and market share become the main focus for pastors, then the next generation votes with their feet and exits congregations. As spiritual leaders, we have got to be better, especially when the church is trying to convince non-believers that Christ's love makes them behave differently than the rest of society. As sociologist of religion Robert Wuthnow observes, the professed *values* of a religious group do not neatly translate into matching public *behaviors* with respect to certain social issues.[84]

Unity matters to God because of our own social witness to outsiders, our ability to do more together, and preparation for heaven. Shared credit and a kingdom mindset are the markers of good partnerships. Here in San Diego's youth ministry world, for example, many of the financial partners who care about outreach to young people simultaneously support FCA, Young Life, UYC and other good organizations that make a positive difference. Sometimes we even go to shared donor meetings because investors like the fact that we work together instead of keeping their dollars separated in lonely silos. Young Life, UYC, and FCA have all brought donors to the same high schools where we serve together. We joke that one week we put the "UYC sign" up, the next week the "Young Life sign" goes up, and the following week it is the "FCA sign." All for the kingdom. We are not hustling anybody because all guests know that our ministries intentionally partner together to benefit students.

Let's Have That "DTR" Talk: Defining the Relationship

After a guy and girl spend a certain amount of time together, a "define the relationship" or "DTR" talk becomes necessary. What are the goals and roles for this relationship? Are we just good friends or boyfriend and girlfriend? How serious are we? Do we have a long-term future? How will we agree to describe this relationship to others in public? These key questions get to the essence of a good DTR conversation. In the same way, it is important to have lots of DTR talks with youth pastors, parachurch workers, students, and campus allies who decide to serve the same schools. We want to clarify roles, expectations, contributions, what the meeting will be called, and what the shared plan is for supporting students in their work on campus.

Unity requires more hard work up front. In the short term it may be easier to work separately. In the long run, however, the labor of unity yields lasting dividends that far exceed what is possible otherwise. I can tell you plainly that our ministry accomplishes far more for kids because we have linked arms with other organizations who bring things to the table that we cannot offer. We need each other. That is the heart and vision behind the Urban Youth *Collaborative*. We need to be comfortable with other people and organizations that are better at certain aspects of ministry than we are. When we let them bring their best, it simultaneously frees us to be the same. To collaborate means to put in hard work and *co-labor* together to accomplish shared kingdom goals. We cannot be threatened by others who are good – and better than us – at what God called them to do.

Scientists who spend time studying light discover it is made up of many colors properly aligned (read: *unified*) along a spectrum. Similarly, in the spiritual world, the light of the world shines brightest when all the colors of the rainbow prism are positioned side by side. This is true of how God designed natural light. It also applies to how he has designed supernatural light (Christ's body) to shine for the world to see. Together we have more to offer students when ministries bring all of their strengths, perspectives, and various gifts to the table. With trust and permission, we can share credit, resources, and dream together with students about what God wants to do at their campus. Through this process, we can rediscover the unity that can be found in comm*unity.*

Reconciling the Most Divided Hour in America

In 1963, the Rev. Dr. Martin Luther King poignantly described the degree of racial segregation evident within the church of his day. While speaking to a group at Western Michigan University he remarked:

> I must admit that I have gone through those moments when I was greatly disappointed with the church and what it has done in this period of social change. We must face the fact that in America, the church is still the most segregated major institution in America. At 11:00 on Sunday morning when we stand and sing that Christ has no east or west, we stand at the most segregated hour of this nation. This is tragic. Nobody of honesty can overlook this.[85]

As an itinerant preacher who guest speaks on Sunday mornings throughout San Diego, I personally feel the pain of knowing Dr. King's declaration still rings true in 2018. I see it Sunday after Sunday when I look out from pulpits across town. I see it Monday through Friday as I visit public schools in my city's different – and often divided – neighborhoods and communities. While we have made great strides from the absolute segregation of the Civil Rights era in the 1960s, no one "of honesty" can deny that the color line still often keeps Anglos and people of other ethnic backgrounds from socializing, working, living, worshiping, and attending school in separate spheres. This produces what Pulitzer Prize winning author David Shipler describes as *A Country of Strangers* between blacks and whites in America. Let me hasten to add that the divide exists between other ethnicities in our nation too. As humans, we are all gifted at finding ways and reasons to separate ourselves from others. We are all good at figuring out how to put ourselves at the center or top of whatever systems we invent or devise.[86] My doctoral dissertation unpacks many of the reasons for these ongoing church divisions from a sociological and theological perspective. I plan to publish parts of that later on. Given the focus and length of this book, however, suffice it to say that all of us (Christians) can do a much better job making our worshipping communities, schools, neighborhoods, and social circles on earth look more like our ultimate shared reality and reconciled destiny in heaven.

I like to joke that heaven may indeed be a gated community, but anyone who believes in Christ will be allowed inside (the gate code is "John316#")! We need to prepare ourselves for that glorious day when the social divisions invented by fallen humans melt away and only our status as God's diverse, redeemed, and infinitely valuable children remains forever. We need to begin recognizing the *imago dei,* or image of God, present in the "other," regardless of tongue, tribe, nationality, or level of affluence. Until that glorious day arrives, our broken and hurting world is dying for a foretaste, a preview, a glimpse, or an approximation of our final home in heaven. Whenever God's people allow this kingdom reality to break through and invade their present circumstances, they offer a gift to an isolated society longing for hope, reconciliation, and unity.

Building Bridges Between Bubbles

An ancient proverb states that fish do not realize there is such a thing as water until they are caught. Up until that pivotal point, they spend their entire lives swimming in water along with all their friends, family, relatives, neighbors, classmates, co-workers, and fellow church goers who often look and live like them. The only way a fish can become aware that water, or anything outside of water exists, is to be caught. Only then do they realize the contrast of something other than what they have always known. The homogeneous subcultural waters many American church attendees live and swim in may not afford many opportunities for relationships outside the pond capable of capturing their imaginations and broadening known life experiences.

Public school engagement, however, is a great way for religious folks to escape the isolation of life in a bubble. At Hoover High School in San Diego, for example, students go home to families that speak over thirty different languages. The urban public school is a microcosm of society where young people must learn to get along with people who are different, disagree respectfully, and find shared goals to work on together. The young and the old can also meet to build relationships on public school grounds. At a recent school clean-up project our organization sponsored, alumni from the classes of 1964 and 1953 worked alongside the football team, current members of Generation Z.[87] This, to me, is a beautiful picture of the kingdom of God! When society's divisions of race, economics, age, and zip codes get overcome as people serve Jesus side by side, I see glimpses of God's eternal kingdom breaking through to our present day.

Another preview of God's kingdom came when our ministry hosted an event called "Bridging Interstate 8." In San Diego County, I-8 runs east to west, effectively cutting the region in half. Generally speaking, wealth and political power can be found in the affluent north while those of us who live in the south often feel as if they must fight to be included in conversations and decisions about resources. In order to bridge this divide, we brought teams of student leaders together from diverse ethnic and geographic backgrounds. We had an African-American group of student leaders come from Lincoln High School in southeast San Diego. Young Latino leaders joined us from Sweetwater High School in our city's South Bay. Anglo student leaders from Cathedral Catholic participated from San Diego's North County, among others.

Some of our ministry's dear friends and supporters hosted the event at their home. Students played games together, participated in several group learning activities about how we see others, and ended the day eating gourmet brick oven pizza from the back of a fire truck (my friend who hosted us has a connection with a renovated fire engine transformed into a mobile pizza kitchen). The best part of the day, though, was the "hot seat." Young leaders could choose to go public with their lives in front of others. From the hot seat, students shared openly about their dreams, struggles, life stories, and what it is like to follow Jesus as a student leader on their campus. After their moment of "outrageous courage" was over, we gathered around them for prayer. It stunned me to see kids from southeast San Diego praying over their peers from North County. It encouraged me to see kids from the South Bay being prayed for by their neighbors to the north from Lincoln High School. Kids from North County "suburbs" prayed earnestly for their peers and new friends who stood for Christ at their inner-city campus. And so on. By the end, everyone walked away realizing that we had far more in common than the differences that make us unique. This special day of understanding, commonality, reconciliation, and unity was a highlight to remember for everyone involved (adults and kids alike). Social capital increases for everyone in Christ's body when we foster kingdom relationships that bridge societal divides.

One Unavoidable Shared Future

We share an unavoidable future destiny in heaven where every tongue, tribe, and nation will stand before the throne of Jesus. Let's get ready! At the end of all this, there will be no church names, no organizational logos, no pastoral egos, just one group of people who know Jesus and another group – cast infinitely far away from the throne – that has nothing to celebrate. If fact, scripture is clear about the opposite destiny awaiting those who pass up Christ's offer to make the payment for our sins. As forgiven and joyful believers, then, we realize our story began in a garden, but it will culminate in a city.[88] According to Revelation 7:9, our future as God's people is multi-ethnic. We all have to overcome our own theological partisanship – when it comes to non-essential doctrines – if we want to experience the unity of God's body.[89] When working together, we ought to display unity in the essentials, liberty in the non-essentials, and in all things charity.[90] UYC does have a Statement of Faith that provides clarity about what we believe to be essential aspects of the Christianity which unites us. Shared commitments about essentials allow us to practice unity amid diversity.

While working together on a school campus, we have to agree to focus on essentials. An outreach campus club may not be the best place for a guest youth pastor or student leader to launch into an eight-part series about why their church believes speaking in tongues is the primary evidence of the Holy Spirit's full presence in someone's life. Similarly, it may not be the place to delve into a four-month treatise on whether predestination and election trumps free choice. When our coalition of Pentecostal, independent, Baptist, Presbyterian, and mini- and mega-churches link arms together on middle and high school campuses, it is for the purpose of supporting student leaders and allowing them to experience Jesus along with their friends. We leave the particular nuances of individual faith traditions for Sunday, mid-week, and small group discussions at local congregations.

Working with public school kids forces church leaders to identify the essentials of the faith that truly matter while breaking them down and explaining God's word in understandable terms – a great discipline for every pastor! If I can keep the attention of a junior high student in a public school, then I can speak to any audience. Talking to kids who are unfamiliar with the gospel keeps me sharp. It forces me to meet relevant needs. I also have to practice distilling the truths of God's word into simple yet accurate terms. As 1 Peter 3:15 reminds us, "Always be prepared to give an answer to everyone who asks you to give the reason for the hope that you have. But do this with gentleness and respect." I am overjoyed any time I get to share about the values of my ultimate true home in heaven and how Jesus' kingdom principles can transform lives and neighborhoods here on earth in a way that reflects where I am "from" and "going." In the meantime – this in-between time – God has entrusted to all of us a ministry of reconciliation (2 Corinthians 5). As this authentically takes place vertically between us and God, it has immediate horizontal implications on how we treat the "other" in communities near and far.[91]

seven

NUTS AND BOLTS:
HOW YOU CAN START TODAY

My heart for this chapter is that you read it more like a menu than a textbook. As your church prayerfully considers building a relationship with a local school, these concrete strategies and best practices can guide – and hopefully inspire – you. No two church and school relationships are exactly the same. There is no cookie-cutter model. It is a living and dynamic process empowered and guided by the Holy Spirit. Look for the providential "sweet spot" where your congregation or organization's resources align with the needs and opportunities presented at a local campus. As you seek God and begin to know who the gatekeepers are on campus, pick one or two things that your congregation can learn to do well. Please do not attempt all of these ideas at once. Start small and grow from there. Like spiritual disciplines in our own lives, simple acts of obedience open up a means of grace for building and deepening relationships with administrators and students. One or two trustworthy channels of connection are all your church needs at first. Focus on "under promising" and "over delivering" when establishing trust with school administrators. When your church's unique resources match up with a particular need or opportunity at a school, you may feel the spark of God ignite a powerful new work inside your congregation.

This is not a step-by-step, "how-to" workbook – that will be published soon – but more of a "why we must" and "what it can look like" book. Through the stories and examples shared throughout, I pray you will be able to discern some transferable principles that point to the "how" along the way. I also recommend finding a campus ministry coach or mentor that can guide you on your specific journey of engaging a school. Should you decide to take the next step, a real person with first-hand experience can help overcome the fear of the unknown and navigate real situations as they arise from relationships with students and administrators. Based on Peter's encounter with Jesus in Luke 5:1-11, I would like to explore practical steps youth workers of all stripes (I define a "youth worker" broadly as any caring adult who positively wants to impact kids) can take to develop effective campus ministry strategies. These are important attitudes for approaching schools – postures of the heart – as well as some practical ideas for action.

Prayerful Surrender

Jesus always wants more of us and is quick to ask for it. When he comes into our lives, he never lets us rest complacently where we are without challenging us to move forward. We see this when he first calls Peter to leave the family fishing business and become transformed into a fisher of men and women. *"Getting into one of the boats, which was Simon's, he asked him to put out a little from the land" (Luke 5:3).* Jesus asked Peter's permission to come aboard and use his boat for a greater purpose. His ordinary fishing craft was suddenly going to serve as the amplification system for Jesus' voice so his words could reach more people. Peter accepted Jesus' invitation to climb in and take his vocation to a new place. As you spend time listening to Jesus' voice through prayer, you may hear him calling you and asking if he can take your youth ministry to a new place. Do you dare to venture out with Jesus into the deeper waters so more people can be reached? Will you let Jesus lead your youth ministry efforts to focus on a local public school campus? Venturing out into deeper and uncharted waters can only happen successfully as Jesus' voice guides us through prayer.

Every Thursday at 6AM, I pray with a teacher who has met with me each week for over twelve years. We first ran into each other back when *The Da Vinci Code* movie came out. Students from the faith club at his high school wanted to spark conversations about the reliability of the Bible with their peers. So the club's leaders put up signs around campus asking the question, "The Da Vinci Code: Is the Bible Reliable?" The posters invited fellow students to come to Room 805 on Thursdays at lunch to discuss the answer. The club leaders then asked me to come and present the case for why the Bible is trustworthy and true. I did this from a theological and sociological (social-scientific) perspective. Based on the movie's premise, however, this particular teacher assumed the meeting would be attempting to prove the Bible is false, riddled with errors, and little more than a package of ancient myths. My friend showed up that first day to debate whoever was presenting so that they would not mislead students by persuading them that the Bible was the biggest con job in the history of the human race. Once he heard my presentation, however, he realized that I was making the case for the Bible's reliability instead of arguing against it. We became fast friends. Since this teacher has the gift of intercessory prayer, we have been meeting to pray about ministry concerns every week since. We meet to talk about what is happening with students on campuses and ask God to intervene. We started by praying for one school. As our ministry has grown, we now pray for over one hundred campuses each week, including new work in Mexico! Our relationship grew together along with the campus outreach. I believe God has assigned this teacher to me, and our ministry, as a personal prayer covering.

Prayer is the only foundation that can undergird a new work of God. While wrestling with a full-time call to campus ministry, I would visit the high school closest to my church to see four students from our youth group during lunch. Two of them looked forward to seeing me. Two others did not want to talk much because it meant "going public" with their faith by admitting they knew a youth pastor in front of their friends. Nonetheless, I made the most of the chance to speak with whoever was interested. Toward the end of the lunch period, I would walk around and pray silently on my way out. God put two distinct prayers on my heart. One sounded familiar, "May your kingdom come and your will be done on earth as it is in heaven." The second one surprised me; I did not fully understand it. "Give me the spiritual keys to this campus," I felt led to pray. So every time I went down the street to the high school nearest to my church, I intentionally prayed these words as I walked passed students in all types of difficult situations. Several years later, the principal ended up giving me a master key to the entire campus. In the spiritual realm, too, I believe that God did the same at this high school. He was poised to open many more doors at this first school and the others that followed. Prayer is the key that unlocks the spiritual and physical doors that God wants you to walk through.

Practicing the Power of Presence

Christ's encounter with Peter continues with Jesus asking him to, *"Put out into the deep and let down your nets for a catch" (v.4)*. In order to be fishers of men and women, we need to go where the fish are. Changing location can change results. Spend time at basketball games, school plays, science fairs, art exhibits, campus clubs, tutoring sessions, assemblies, leadership classes, study hall, detention, and anywhere students are. Leading with presence and service makes our eventual words more powerful. As Young Life brilliantly teaches, your faithful presence "earns the right to be heard."

I live down the street from Lincoln High School in the south-east section of inner-city San Diego. When I first started UYC, the school got leveled to the ground for a remodel. The year it reopened, a double homicide ended the lives of two kids and shook the community and student body to the core. Shots rang out. Two young bodies lay in caskets. I will never forget the morning I showed up on the first day of school after the incident. A huddled mass of students had been shuffled into a large open classroom by administrators. No one seemed to be giving direction to the "meeting." Full of shock and grief, these resilient young people struggled to make sense of what had unexpectedly happened to their friends and classmates. As I stood there, several students began writing an impromptu sign asking for donations for the family who lost their child. Tragically, it costs quite a bit to die. Compounding the loss, families in my community often struggle to afford the expenses of a headstone, burial plot, casket, mortician services, and all the other medical fees associated with a loved one passing away. Since the incident was publicized in the media, several other community leaders showed up at the school that day too. The mayor's gang commissioner stood nearby me. A local business leader also came to pay their respects and attempt to comfort students. I give them credit for being there. As they talked and gave their credentials, however, the kids stared down blankly at their desks. When it was my turn to speak, I simply said, "Hi, my name is Nate and quite a few of you have seen me around because I help support the weekly Bible club that meets here on campus." Every head in the room suddenly lifted up and stared at me. My greatest credential in that moment of pain was that I cared enough about them to be there faithfully. I had other credentials that I could have mentioned. But none of those mattered if I did not care enough to meet them consistently on their turf. It's one thing to appear at a school when the news trucks pull up out front. It is quite another to demonstrate that students matter by predictably being present on their turf before and after the cameras roll.

Practically speaking, being there allows the "word to become flesh" and dwell among us (John 1). Christ chose to leave his throne in heaven, become human, and journey to earth. He decided we are worth leaving all the glory behind. So he went after us. He learned our language, discovered our culture, became part of our community, loved sinners, walked among us, and showed us what wholeness and life in the kingdom was all about. Incarnational ministry, then, means being consistently present at a school to whatever degree a campus allows adult guests. Some volunteers find meaningful roles that allow them to serve on a daily basis. Options can include anything from hall monitors, to crossing guards, to tutors, to volunteer security guards. Once trust is established, relationships can lead to open doors. After school hours are a great time to attend games, plays, recitals, and other campus events. For teenagers experiencing a changing cast of principals, coaches, teachers, friends, boyfriends, and even dads, a consistent and trustworthy adult makes a big impression. Kids do not care how much we know until they know how much we care. We demonstrate our care by simply showing up. Several senior pastors connected to UYC have been involved at the same campus for over ten years! This gives them a considerable pool of credibility and trust when speaking into the lives of students and administrators alike. Their track record of humble and effective service earns respect and gives them the ability to respond to unique crises and joys that come up each school year.

Casting a Broader Vision for Youth Ministry

Instead of focusing only on the children of parents who tithe, it is important for senior pastors and youth pastors to cast vision within the congregation about God's heart for lost students outside the household of faith. "Without vision," the Proverbs say, "the people perish."[92] Without the vision for reaching out to public schools from the senior pastor, the people who end up perishing are often the students who go to school down the street from the church. The senior pastor may not have time to be personally involved at a nearby school directly, but the pastor needs to "bless" the idea and empower the youth pastors or ministry team to make campus ministry a priority for the congregation. Instead of outsourcing the idea to the youth pastor alone, senior pastors can take the opportunity to involve members of the congregation, youth ministry team, parents, grandparents, and other volunteers from the community. We have seen churches get "saved" and "born again" by leaving the four walls of their building and engaging in their surrounding community. Reaching out to a school down the street is a powerful strategy to see transformation in the lives of congregation members as well as others on the outside. One senior pastor who guest speaks faithfully at a local high school club tells me it is his favorite time of the week. "The grown-ups I talk to on Sundays," he tells me, "they are already set in their ways." The young people he gets to address on Thursdays at lunch, however, are "still charting their course" and have not made up their minds yet. As a senior pastor, he decided there is no better audience than a group of student leaders who invite him to share God's side of the story with friends over lunch at the public school.

Passion for the Lost

As we saw earlier, a miraculous catch of fish changed Peter's life forever. After he obeyed Jesus, he discovered Christ's power to alter reality. *"And when they had done this, they enclosed a large number of fish, and their nets were breaking" (v. 6).* Peter used to stay up all night doing whatever it took to catch fish in his own strength. His encounter with Jesus gave him a new assignment and a new passion: fishing for men and women with different means because they needed to be caught. Just like Peter would experience later after his Pentecost sermon, Christ is sending people into the oceans of humanity with a passion for seeing people cross over from one reality to the next, from death away from Christ to life to the fullest with him. He went after Peter because the rock of the church was going to catch lots of lost fish that needed to be rescued from their current environment. In order to be effective in campus ministry, we must let Jesus go after us so he can impart his passion for the lost inside our souls. If we lack passion for the lost, Jesus can change us. He did not only call youth pastors to care for previously caught fish in the youth group tank, although the tank does need cleaning. He calls us deep into the ocean to fish for new men and women that he desperately wants on board. Let Jesus share this passion with you!

Some of my academic and progressive Christian friends might object and say that I am demeaning the young people I write about by describing them as lost. "You assume they have something lacking. You undervalue and look down on them judgmentally when you talk that way," they might say. On the contrary, I think that going after someone that is lost demonstrates a person's indispensable value. Have you ever lost your wallet, keys, or kid? Don't you stop everything, turn the house upside down, and mobilize everyone imaginable in the search? And then, when you find what is lost, don't you breathe a sigh of relief and celebrate when something critical to life gets found again? When Jesus tells the parables of the lost coin, the lost sheep, and the lost prodigal son, he is not doing so to look down on the lost.[93] Instead, he demonstrates that they are so valuable that it is worth stopping and leaving everything else until what's lost is found again. Each community and family is not the same without the missing person. Life is incomplete without them. We *noticed* they were gone! They matter so much that we have to go after them. God wants his kids back! He runs to meet them and embrace them. That's why there is more rejoicing over the one that was lost than over the others that did not need to be found again.

Partnering Together

As mentioned earlier, the task of fishing for men and women at public schools is too big to succeed alone. *"They signaled to their partners in the other boat to come and help them" (v.7).* Peter had to call for partners to help him or else the nets would break and the fish would be lost. If you are reading these words and seriously considering campus ministry, please do not just wing it and show up on a campus alone tomorrow at lunch. See who else is out there that you can call, ride along with, meet for coffee, or ask to walk alongside you to help teach you the ropes of campus ministry. There are lots of excellent groups to meet: Young Life, Urban Youth Collaborative, Fellowship of Christian Athletes, National School Project, First Priority, and other local churches and organizations that have successfully "cracked" the campus ministry code. They would be eager to meet you and walk with you. Learn from them and set out together.

Congregational Training and Networking

To make partnering together easier, we host pastors and youth pastors who support student-led clubs at public school campuses at a quarterly gathering. We share best practices, eat some really good food, encourage each other, strengthen our relationships, and pray for God to bless the young people in our city. We call this gathering the UYC Late Lunch Learning Lab, or "Late Lunch" for short. It has been inspiring to see churches from all denominations, sizes, ethnicities, and zip codes come together for the sake of youth in San Diego. By sharing successes and struggles together, we have gotten better at the task of supporting students and administrators on campuses. Occasionally we feature a national speaker, but most of the presenters are local practitioners who convey strategies for effectively coming alongside students on campus.

Position Yourself to Serve

As church folk, we can be guilty of making the well-meaning – yet naïve – assumption that we know what other people need. Instead of coming in with our own predetermined agenda, it can be more effective to ask a simple yet powerful question, "How can we help?" Meeting practical needs identified by students, coaches, and administrators lets those we come to serve set the agenda. As mentioned in the previous chapters, physical and spiritual ministry goes well together. A student who is hungry for daily bread may not be able to receive a message about any spiritual "bread of life" until the first type of hunger gets satisfied. Similarly, a student who struggles to read at grade level will not only have trouble engaging in history class, but he will also have difficulty interacting with scripture. Addressing the former type of literacy makes the latter possible too. Caring for students as whole people means we must be concerned with their bodies, minds, and spirits as interconnected parts of personhood. God does not divide us up into compartmentalized and fractured creatures. He wants each person to experience the wholeness of shalom. Our ministry to young people must also be holistic.

Sports Clubs at School

Asking good questions led one youth pastor on a great adventure at an "alternative" continuation high school for kids who previously got expelled from other traditional schools. While working with students who built a resume of past trouble, this youth pastor discovered that the world of sports is a great place to develop relationships with students. By practicing and playing together, he learned to affirm their potential and communicate that their personal value did not decrease due to previous missteps. Since the school was located just a few blocks from this youth pastor's church, he became speaking regularly in the campus' "town hall" meetings, a motivational pep-talk that gathered and focused the community of faculty and students together to start each new day. As the relationship with students, teachers, and administrators grew, the youth pastor noticed that the Friday "sports club" on campus had only one ball and one cone to work with. The faithful yet petite substitute teacher overseeing the club had a difficult time managing the group of large burly guys. Since the youth pastor had a gym full of sports equipment at his church and a team of athletic college interns, he offered to come alongside the sports club to provide some support and resources. The school quickly accepted.

The first day was rough. Expelled kids tend to play soccer more aggressively than others might choose to. One of the students did a slide tackle to take out the goalie (one of the church's college interns) in order to "score" a goal. The intern quickly informed the student that knocking over the goalie is against the rules and therefore the goal did not count. This information did not sit well with the student who proceeded to make threats against the church volunteers! I'll never forget the day the continuation school called to inform me that "volunteers from your organization received death threats at our campus today." They felt a certain duty to inform me. I have never received a call quite like that before or since then!

The church did not give up. They kept going back to support the sports club week after week. Soon death threats gave way to high fives as students realized that the volunteers genuinely cared for them. Seven students eventually joined the church's indoor soccer league and the congregation put on a BBQ for the school to celebrate graduates at the end of the academic year. Years later, the church's youth pastor was nominated as "Volunteer of the Year" and served on the search committee that helped select the new principal. Faculty members began opening up to the youth pastor about their personal lives and asked for a listening ear and guidance. During Christmas of the first semester, the principal invited me to share about the historical origins of the holiday because he thought it would be a "good educational exercise" if the students knew the background of that tradition. I shared the story of Jesus' family getting turned away from all the hotels in town. Then, I explained that Jesus knows what it is like to be kicked out of places when you wanted to be included. I told them that Jesus will not turn away anyone who seeks him out this Christmas season. For an audience that all got kicked out of traditional school, these kids could particularly relate to Jesus' story and experience during the first Christmas.

Serving Football, Basketball, and Baseball Teams

We have equipped six youth pastors to volunteer as "chaplains" for high school football teams, basketball squads, and one baseball team throughout San Diego. They provide pre-game meals, share motivational pep-talks, and support students through whatever life hits them with during the season. Anything can happen! I have seen a player make it to the practice squad of the Jacksonville Jaguars. I have officiated the funeral for a player whose nine-week old baby died of SIDS (Sudden Infant Death Syndrome). And everything in between. Being part of students' lives on their turf opens up the possibility for transformative relationships that would not be possible otherwise. My church and other congregational partners have hosted countless year-end banquets for football teams and basketball teams. One year, at a school-wide meeting for coaches and parents from all sports, the athletic director at one high school went so far as to introduce our senior pastor and me as "the pastors to our school." This was a title he voluntarily came up with to describe what he saw God doing. This past July, I was blessed to do pre-marital counseling and officiate the wedding of two coaches at a local high school where we serve. They asked me to perform their wedding after journeying together and supporting students for many years. It was a true honor to see God weaving our stories together. By sharing life, I get to experience all the joys and sorrows that students and adults invite me into. Being on campus allows many new adventures to unfold. As relationships build and trust grows, God often takes his work off of the field and deeper into the lives of students, coaches, and teachers.

Job Training & Shadowing

When a young person decides to follow Jesus, they will get to experience heaven when they die. But the "life to the fullest" promised by Christ also has to involve something meaningful to do between ages 15 and 75. Students need access to training, role models, and career paths they can aspire to. Business leaders can mentor young people in a specific profession through job shadow days, internships, and on-the-job training. Through these experiences, youth develop life skills and can become passionate about pursuing a particular career. On the flip side, business leaders in a congregation can build a relationship with a young person from a different demographic background that enriches their life and expands their horizons as well. This type of cross-mentoring relationship can prove equally transformative for the young person and the professional alike. During our next season of ministry, we are working to develop entrepreneurial opportunities for young people who want job experience, life skills, and Christian discipleship centered around the workplace. Our goal is to see more young leaders like Andrue Didiavong (featured in this book) live out their dreams to be small-business owners by using their gifts to glorify God. His Christian apparel company, "AG2G" (All Glory to God), captures this concept beautifully! We would like to invite established Christian business owners and professionals from various fields to come alongside young entrepreneurs for mentoring in their vocation and discipleship in their personal faith. We see those twin goals going hand in hand. Young people needs tools for – and role models of – success in this life and for eternity.

Tutoring

When our church first started working with the varsity football team at San Diego High School twelve years ago, they had eighteen academically ineligible players on the team who could not keep a 2.0 GPA. As mentioned earlier, it takes discipline – if you ask me – to keep your grades that low in SDUSD. In order to help, our senior pastor connected the team with some volunteer tutors through the military. They provided academic assistance to players so they could get their grades up. This amounted to a real boost for the team as well as the individuals who started to gain competency in their coursework.

Research shows that children who do not know how to read by third grade are at significantly higher risk of negative behaviors and undesirable life outcomes in the future. Kids that do not hit this key educational milestone become four times more likely to drop out of high school.[94] Literacy also leads to a life with higher earning potential and lower risks of crime or prison time.[95] Despite all the big advantages – and significant pitfalls – hinging on this critical cut-off for early childhood literacy, only 35% of US fourth graders are proficient in reading.[96] *If a few committed local church volunteers could sit and read with a second grader for an hour or two every week, they could literally change a child's life!* This is the simple and powerful truth of literacy that more people of faith must embrace. It is easy to make a profound difference. As a literacy specialist, my late mom was very passionate about kids learning to read early in life because it profoundly charts their course in one direction or the other.

Many schools already have reading or tutoring programs available where church volunteers can join in. If not, work with the school to start one. During the tutoring sessions on campus, it is important to realize this is not a time to "proselytize" or talk about Jesus overtly. We cannot practice "bait and switch" tactics. Relationships of trust will develop with school officials when they see we understand the rules and can keep our promises. We need to know the boundaries and stick to them. Reading with students on campus is a *different* legal space from the student-led faith clubs described elsewhere in this book. Both spaces create valuable opportunities for enriching students' lives in different ways. Since both types of spaces exist on public school campuses (limited open forums and closed forums), it is important for people of faith to know the difference and have resources for making a positive contribution in both environments within a public school context. As relationships with students grow, there may be other opportunities for conversation that develop as a result of tutoring. Yet we must respect the initial arrangement that the school has invited us into. If a church wanted to offer an after-school reading and tutoring site off campus where students could gather to do homework, get academic support, and hang out in a safe environment, then this would be an acceptable way to blend studying with some faith content.

Backpack Drives & School Supplies

Backpacks, grocery gift cards, clothing, school supplies, and other items represent constant needs for students and schools, particularly in an urban environment. Since district and family budgets are often tight, practical items go a long way and show love in a tangible fashion. *A teacher friend of mine recently retired. When I asked what changes he will enjoy in this new chapter of life, he told me he looked forward to the personal savings from not having to buy hundreds of dollars' worth of classroom supplies out of his own pocket every month!* Whenever a church can provide pens, pencils, paper, notebooks, erasers, glue, scissors, markers, construction paper, and other items, this is an easy win for everyone. Students get blessed with supplies they really need, and churches earn favor with administrators and teachers too. It is important for these gifts to be given at face value, and simply because we care, with no strings attached. Coordinating a school supply or backpack drive makes for another great "first date" between a church and a school. Usually this type of arrangement can be set up directly with the principal, vice principal, a counselor, or the athletic director, depending on the campus. The conversation can start by simply asking the question, "What do you need?" Once the campus gatekeeper notices that we follow through, keep our word, and deliver, then they may begin to trust us with deeper needs or bigger opportunities as the relationship develops over time.

Mediation & Conflict Resolution

Several years ago, a racially-motivated fight broke out between Latino and African-American students at a campus where we serve. The school went into lockdown and law enforcement officers responded with a heavy police presence along with a SDPD helicopter. After the incident, one school administrator suggested that a city councilmember should come and speak with the young people involved on both sides of the conflict. The principal, however, said, "Why should we call an elected official that the kids do not know personally?" She went on to say, "Let's call Pastor Pete

[Contreras] who has been working with our school and students for many years." So the school set up a twelve-week intervention and mediation program during class time. Pastor Pete Contreras, the lead pastor at my church, facilitated learning activities where both sides developed tools for listening, understanding the other, offering forgiveness, practicing mutual respect, and developing conflict resolution skills. All parties involved gained new capacities for relating to others who are different. Instead of mass expulsions, the incident led to personal growth and a heightened mutual respect between racial groups on campus. Students who completed this conflict resolution class were far less likely to get swept up in ethnically-motivated strife again because they learned to see the "other" as someone of equal value who is worthy of respect and love.

School Beautification Projects

For the past nine years, our ministry has partnered with other churches and community organizations to put on a large-scale annual "School Beautification Day" throughout San Diego County. Each August, up to 1,000 faith-based volunteers join together from local churches to do meaningful facility and infrastructure work at twenty-five to forty campuses depending on the summer. These labors of love communicate non-verbally that students matter when they return in the fall. Mobilizing a group of churches to pull weeds, paint benches, mulch, install sprinklers, do light or heavy construction, garden, remove trash, or other tangible projects makes for another great "first date" encounter between a church and school. The scale of the project can vary based on a church's expertise and resources. Some congregations – such as Pathways Church in Santee, California – have many professional contractors who attend worship services. This allows them work with their school districts to take on large technical projects that require skilled labor and heavy equipment. One year they drove a huge two-person crane onto an east county San Diego campus. They successfully moved a five-ton boulder from the back to the front of a local high school! I jokingly told them that they were showing off because no other church can rival their impressive and sophisticated work. Afterwards, it looked like the hand of God came down to move that rock. In reality, God sent his people to do it.

In an era of ongoing budget challenges, administrators greatly appreciate the assistance that churches offer when it comes to beautification work. With enough advance notice, unions can approve volunteer work when it is negotiated ahead of time, supervised by their people, and only happens once per year. This lowers the perceived threat level to the point that union bosses can tolerate – and occasionally get excited about – the idea. The custodial and maintenance workers themselves appreciate the chance to direct an army of dedicated volunteers who tackle projects that they simply cannot get to. In some districts we serve, trash and weeds build up to the point that they become unmanageable due to limited gardening crews. Overall, school officials have no unfounded fears of "proselytizing" because the events usually happen on Saturday and we are mainly working with a bench or a flower bed (both are difficult to "convert"). While laboring together, principals and pastors discover the value in having each other around. A painted door can become an open door for future projects, opportunities, and relationships throughout the school year and beyond.

Motivational School Assemblies

Imagine a school gymnasium or auditorium packed with a thousand students gathered for an inspirational message about overcoming life's big obstacles and achieving their dreams. Some campuses arrange for back-to-back assemblies so the message can get out to the entire student body on the same day. It is possible – and worthwhile – to host a program like this with a school if done correctly. The delivery has to be high energy, interactive, multi-media, and enthusiastic in order to hold the attention of young people who are *required* to come by their principal. By the time the program gets started, however, almost *everyone* – including teachers – is thrilled that we got them out of class for an hour or more. Content for these programs must be *non-religious* since the principal requires attendance, adults are leading, and the event happens during class time. Bible talks or prayers do not work in this environment. The presentations communicate important life principles like: "The five friends you have now will be the sum total of your future;" "What you sow now you will reap later;" "There is an important dream inside you that the world needs;" "You do not have to be defined by your past;" or "Your words have power to build people up or to tear them down." Administrators of all stripes agree that kids have limitless value and possess a world of potential. We can all agree that homework is better than "putting in work" with a gang. Graduating is better than dropping out. Using words to heal is better than using them to destroy. Achieving dreams is better than letting them die.

For many years, our organization has partnered with a national school assembly team called iThink Big (www.ithinkbig.org) because they are among the best presenters in the US. Another top-quality school assembly speaker is Gabe Salazar (www.gabe-salazar.com) who has also worked with us successfully as the host of Project 25 for the past two years. We have solidified relationships with school administrators and then sponsored an assembly team to come in and share with the whole school. Students leave encouraged, inspired, and passionate about making a positive difference in their communities. They can also tailor-make an assembly to focus on anti-bullying, suicide, drug and alcohol prevention, or other specific topics school administrators identify as relevant. In many cases, students and youth pastors from the community can participate in the assemblies when they learn to "code switch" and share pre-screened, non-religious messages.

Depending on the principal's perspective, student leaders from the school's Christian club – since they are the group helping to host the assembly – are allowed to do a "shout out" inviting any interested kids to attend their optional student-led meeting. At each campus, we always honor the principal's preference as to whether such an announcement may be made. Coming together for an exhilarating session that emphasizes the great potential inside each young person makes for an unforgettable assembly! The presentation concludes by inviting students to come forward and write down obstacles they face on a stack of cinder blocks. These moments allow students to identify real pain and challenges in their lives. Comments include messages and trauma from their past, statements about self-worth, fears about the future, relationship goals, family financial challenges, and health concerns for loved ones. Reading the list often requires tissues and follow-up with particular students. We also work with counselors to respond when certain issues arise in students' lives. Then, on behalf of all kids in attendance, the assembly presenters ask everyone to stand as they break through the stack of bricks to symbolize that it is possible to push through hard circumstances. Since we pay the bill for these presentations (a $1,500 value per assembly), there is no cost to a school. Administrators are grateful and often accept the offer. Over the past nine years, UYC has hosted more than one hundred assembly presentations for well over 100,000 young people.

As I write, we have just launched a new partnership with a ministry organization in Mexico to offer assemblies to an additional fifteen thousand students each year in Tijuana, Mexicali, Tecate, Rosarito, and Ensenada. We are hoping this will eventually spread throughout the entire nation of Mexico. We are excited to learn from our new partner across the border and share productive assembly strategies that we have discovered in the US too. Regardless of the country, all students speak the language of love. Quality assemblies bring the entire community of adults and students together around their shared commitment to seeing students experience life to the fullest.

Summer Camps

Each July, our ministry partners with the Fellowship of Christian Athletes (FCA) to take 150 students to UCLA for a week of sports camp. During this transformative experience, students live on campus, eat in the cafeteria, sleep in the dorms, practice their sport in the Bruins facilities, and gather for worship during the evening chapel services in Pauley Pavilion where the Bruin basketball teams play. Joining a thousand young people from all over Southern California for worship every night makes for an unforgettable trip. Students benefit athletically, spiritually, and academically since the dream of higher education suddenly feels more accessible after living on campus. Thanks to FCA's generosity, our students receive $75,000 worth of scholarships to cover the majority of the costs of camp each summer. Kids we serve come from backgrounds that make the standard $595 registration fee inaccessible. Years ago, FCA's Southern California Director, Colin Sinclair, made a deal with me. "You find the kids," he said, "we'll find the cash." I prayed for about two-and-a-half seconds before accepting his offer!

Our ministry has been inviting hundreds of kids to camp every summer and bankrupting Colin ever since. I praise God for this kingdom partnership and the thousands of changed lives that have resulted from it over the years!

I am overwhelmed and humbled by the incredible ministry partners like Colin that God has brought to me. We are always looking for people who have a kingdom heart and love to see young people from all backgrounds experience the athletic, spiritual, and academic benefits of camp. Other youth pastors and organizations often have their own unique camp experiences that they can also offer interested students. Whether it is through a local church youth ministry, Young Life, Youth for Christ, or another opportunity, summer camp provides a time away from the noise and pressures of their neighborhood. Young people from public schools have an opportunity to examine their life, forge meaningful new friendships, and – if they listen closely – they often hear the voice of God calling their name. We encourage all church partners to find a summer camp opportunity for kids so everyone can stay connected between each school year.

Persevere and Count the Cost

Be ready to count the cost of campus ministry. *"And when they had brought their boats to land, they left everything and followed him"* *(v.10-11).* There will still be sleepless nights of toil that feel frustrating. Your senior pastor may not fully understand – right away or ever. You may encounter resistance from certain parents, people on campus, or in the community. You may have days where you feel tired, worn out, and wonder if you are really making a difference. There will be financial strains. You may even get flak from a few administrators and even other Christian groups in town that do not understand what God has called you to do. Yet if you persevere and continue following Jesus, you and your partners will begin catching people from death unto life... You may even witness a catch that is "astonishing" to all who see it! I have also found that some critics can be won over by witnessing our faithful love, prayer, and fruitful service over the long haul.

Following Through and Keeping Your Word

Several years ago, the principal at an inner-city school convened a group of local senior pastors for a monthly "informational meeting" about the campus. In all my years of campus ministry, I had never seen a senior school administrator – who was interestingly undecided with respect to his own personal faith – open up a regular channel of communication with local pastors so effectively. This particular school struggled with periodic behavioral issues and some students were inconsistent when it came to getting to class on time. The principal asked this team of pastors – not affiliated with our organization – if they could come by during passing periods or lunch to serve as positive role models who kept kids safe. The principal specifically wanted help encouraging students and directing them toward their next class. I distinctly remember several of the pastors taking photos of the gathering because they were so taken with the opportunity to meet in the "inner sanctum" of the principal's large private conference room. To my knowledge, few if any of the pastors showed up consistently to take the principal up on his offer. Despite several follow-up emails requesting assistance for the fifteen-acre campus which had limited security guards, the group of pastors failed to follow through beyond their monthly meetings. They were more interested in the photo opportunity than the chance to roll up their sleeves and make a difference.

Learning the Law

As stated in Chapter 3, knowing the law is an important aspect of campus ministry. Many administrators, teachers, parents, students, and pastors are unaware of the substantial religious liberties afforded to students and their guests through the US Constitution and Equal Access Act. A good civil liberties attorney can help your church understand the legal boundaries when working with public schools. As a helpful reference tool, I have included a two-page, bullet-point summary of legal rights for faith-based clubs on campuses in the Appendix. This was written by our attorney, Dean Broyles, of the National Center of Law and Policy. Our ministry uses this helpful document to clarify the law as we advise students, campus allies, churches, and administrators in our city. All laws described in this document are federal, therefore they apply to public schools in every US city, suburban area, or rural context.

Learning A New Language

Effective cross-cultural leaders learn how to "code switch," which can be defined as comfortably going back and forth — with quickness and agility — between two different languages or cultures. Often this involves deciphering subtle but important customs, values, and nuances present in each context. When relating to their audience and conversation partners, religious people engaging in the public square must learn to speak the language of the administration and students. This does not mean we are deceptive or hide who we are. It simply means we must learn to *translate* what we do into the language of those we work with. By looking for *shared goals and values*, we can emphasize projects and objectives that all parties can agree on. As mentioned earlier, every administrator wants kids graduating more, engaging with gangs less, participating in community service more, bullying less, growing in self-esteem, decreasing in high-risk behaviors, recognizing their own high value as a person, thinking less about conflict with others, focusing on hope, ignoring distractions, gaining skills, losing hang-ups, discovering their gifts, forgetting their critics, and achieving their full – what we know to be God-given – potential. Responding to shared opportunities and needs for the sake of students can turn church leaders and administrators into meaningful partners who pursue the well-being of a community's children together.

Learning a new language also requires us to know the boundaries of speech in various contexts on campus. To review, what a pastor is allowed to say when invited as a guest speaker to a student-led Christian club is very different than what is allowed when speaking at an all-school assembly. As mentioned earlier, the legal parameters for those gatherings are very different. It is important to know the rules and play by the rules so administrators can trust you. Christian workers should develop skills that allow them to share something worth saying in both settings without getting kicked off of campus. Often, I pause for a split second as I translate my message for different audiences. Like Paul, we are called to "become all things to all people" so that others can encounter Christ.[97]

When speaking with young people who are un(der)exposed to church, it becomes vital that we use words that they can understand. Avoid high context Christian (read: *"Christianese"*) terms that require technical definitions. At first, these phrases remain foreign to the coming generation. For example, telling a young person that "Christ's substitutionary atonement propitiates our iniquity before God the Father" will likely make us sound crazy. Although the previous statement is true and theologically precise, it makes no sense unless it gets translated. But sharing that "Jesus made the way for us to get back into a right relationship with

God" could become a beautiful starting point for a life-changing conversation. As God's ambassadors across generations and cultures, we must learn the communication skills needed to accurately and compassionately represent the kingdom of God to the nations, school districts, young people, and neighborhoods he has called us to. The universal language of love – when expressed in practical ways – makes the gospel message difficult to resist. Christ's unthinkable sacrifice of himself makes the opportunity for salvation available to everyone who repents and receives him as master.

Grief Counseling & Crisis Response

Several years ago, soon after an exciting motivational assembly at San Ysidro Middle School, I got a call from the principal. "I don't know if you have been following the news," he began, "but one of our students was killed execution-style in Mexico over the weekend." He went on to tell me how masked gunmen stormed into a family reunion, demanded that women and children go into one room while they ordered the men into the kitchen. Juan (name changed), a fourteen-year-old eighth-grade student at the school, thought it was a joke. So he went with the men into the kitchen and lost his life with other men in the family after being shot at point blank range. His dad played dead and was the only man who survived. "Can you please come back to our school on Thursday to officiate a memorial service?" the principal asked. I could not say no. So I gathered some other clergy from the community and we helped facilitate a memorial service for this young man with his family sitting in the front row. We returned to the same gym where – only a week earlier – we had just been sharing high fives with students and celebrating their potential. This was literally the same school, the same day of the week, the same assembly hall, *with one less person*. He was sorely missed. The superintendent, many district principals, parents, and students, all gathered to pay their respects. Everyone was trying to make sense out of what just happened: a precious young life got cut tragically short.

I wish I could say that these events are rare in our ministry. But each year UYC pastors get called on to respond to some type of disturbance, walkout, or death that touches the campus and the broader community. Whether a suicide, homicide, or unrest on campus, our team of pastors have considerable credibility and relationships to draw upon when caring for students and administrators in times of crisis. In those moments, school administrators and students know they need spiritual resources from the faith community in order to care for the people entrusted to them.

When memorial services happen on school grounds, the content has to be modified. Yet the opportunity to share love, comfort, hope, to grieve together, and celebrate the gift of life constitutes a privilege I will never pass up. Later, this same principal confided that he tried to reach several other pastors before he contacted me. All of them wanted to charge a large honorarium, or officiating fee, if they were to come to the school for a memorial service that day. The principal – leading a school in one of San Diego's poorest communities through an unimaginable tragedy– literally could not afford their services. "Then," he told me, "your card fell out of my folder." He recalled that we did not charge him for school beautification days or the motivational assembly we did together. He knew we would be willing to help with no mention of a bill. How could any pastor turn down an opportunity to care for middle school students in such a deep time of need? Our responsiveness led to a deeper relationship with the administration. Later we saw students leading a Bible club on their campus and inviting a local church youth pastor as a guest. These meetings drew ninety-five students a week for the rest of that school year.

Three Potential Paths Forward

When it comes to practically getting started, we have discovered three potential paths forward when looking to take the first step of campus ministry. It goes without saying that all of these steps – before, during, and after – require constant discernment and prayer. Track one involves supporting young leaders who are interested in starting a student-led Christian club on their middle or high school campus. This process entails identifying motivated students, finding a faculty advisor, completing the application with the student government, and picking a day, time, and room for the meeting. Since these meetings are student-led, occur during non-instructional time (before school, at lunch, or after school), kids can invite their friends and may also invite guest speakers from local congregations. If students would like to do so, they can also let attendees know about off-campus church opportunities for interested friends who attend the lunch meeting.

Secondly, if you do not have students in your church at a particular school, you can pursue non-religious acts of service as a starting point. Good deeds build good will, which lays the foundation to share the good news.[98] In this book, we have listed lots of strategies that our church partners have successfully used here in San Diego. Instead of trying to master them all, find one or two that align your congregation's resources with the needs, opportunities, and dreams of a campus. By loving students and schools with no strings attached, we can see one met need lead to another and eventually bigger dreams and projects can be accomplished. As trust grows, so do the opportunities to expand the work on campus. Effective ministry at one school, in turn, can become a model and reference point for work at new campuses. In every case, quality matters more than quantity. We will unknowingly reproduce our strengths as well as our blind spots. So it pays to take our time, get feedback, and continue to improve over time. As Mother Teresa said, the exact type of work we do does not matter as much as "how much love we put into it."[99]

Finally, if you do not have students in your church at a particular school and have no viable avenues for non-religious acts of service, you can pursue a facility rental agreement. This would be the same as a church renting a school for Sunday worship services but instead your congregation or organization would rent a classroom to run a club on a weekday after school. Under this arrangement, the club would not need to be student-led or have a faculty member present. If the school rents to any other outside organization, by law they cannot refuse to rent to a Christian organization on the basis of the group's religious affiliation. This legal reality has been tested all way up to the Supreme Court, which set a strong precedent for non-discrimination and equal opportunities for religious groups to rent public school facilities.[100] Plus, it is highly affordable. Most of our facility rental agreements only cost ten dollars per classroom for an entire school year. This avenue is definitely worth pursuing as a possibility in a district near you.

Reaping the Rewards

Sharing life on a public school campus opens up doors to experience the joys and sorrows of students' lives. My heart has been through a roller coaster of events that pulled, shaped, broke, and thrilled me in new and irreversible ways. Even the deepest tragedies can produce great fruit as Jesus brings beauty out of ashes.

When God's people are trusted enough to be invited into a crisis, powerful opportunities for ministry ensue. As followers of Jesus, we must be like our master who weeps with those who mourn and rejoices with those who celebrate. When we enter into the dead, dark, scary places that some religious people dare not venture, Christ transforms those around us by speaking words of resurrection life through our lips. If the contemporary church wants to reach the next generation, we must learn to weep, go, and speak as Jesus did. Taking risks is unavoidably built into following Jesus. Overcoming the fear of the unknown is an important part of getting started in campus ministry. Plan on being occasionally misunderstood, periodically discouraged, and frequently inspired! If you hit a roadblock or an unexpected challenge, do not face it alone. Reach out to someone who can understand and walk with you through the process. That is what UYC is here for! The next generation is counting on you to find a way to support, encourage, and equip them to lead. If we see the church as an agent of the kingdom of God, we will be less concerned about whether young people get into our particular church and much more interested in whether they find a solid Christ-centered spiritual home somewhere. Investing in youth outreach may not translate into an immediate boon in new tithing families, but the gains in God's kingdom and in eternity could be substantial.

eight

A PICTURE OF THE FUTURE

I magine a future where shalom spreads more fully throughout America's cities! I dream of a day when pastors get together regularly in communities across the US without being motivated primarily by a fleeting political campaign, ballot initiative, crisis response, or an outsider's cause promoting temporary "unity." What if God's people created positive and unified change from within the systems and communities where they already live? What if believers in Jesus became known for what we are *for* more than what we are *against*? I dream of a day when supporting a school becomes as normal for churches as hosting weekly worship services. If you would like to make this happen, experiment in the kingdom, or go deeper in your existing work with students at public schools, then we would love to hear from you.

Our nation is witnessing a decline in the number of young people that profess classic Christian values, live a moral lifestyle, possess basic biblical literacy, and espouse a Christian worldview. Of high school students who do hold such convictions and their accompanying behaviors, a significant percentage of them end up discarding their faith upon entering college.[101] This book makes the case that public school campuses are the place where the future of our nation – and the spiritual well-being of its students – will be decided. The vast majority of young people who come to faith in Jesus – up to 94% according to some researchers – do so by age 18.[102] As an evangelist, these spiritual realities make graduation ceremonies bitter-sweet occasions for me. On one hand, I am so proud of the accomplishments of each young person, I celebrate their achievements, and wish them the absolute best as they launch into an exciting and unknown future. On the other hand, statistically, I know that many have already decided their eternal destiny when they walk across the stage to grab their high school diploma. The church can make a difference for many young people who are hungry for meaning, belonging, purpose, direction, forgiveness, and value. Their gifts are needed in the kingdom. Our society will benefit from engaged young leaders who know why they are on planet Earth and have the courage to live out bold God-given dreams for their communities.

The public school campus is a microcosm of America's bigger pluralistic society where people must learn to disagree respectfully, love those who are different, serve everyone, and passionately yet humbly make the case for what they believe. According to researcher George Barna, of the two generations older than current middle and high school students, only 4% of millennials and 7% of Generation-Xers have what he describes as a "biblical worldview."[103] "We are in a crisis," Barna asserts. "If the Church does not wake up and solve it, biblical Christianity in the United States is in jeopardy."[104] In order for these trends to reverse, local congregations must prioritize campus ministry and empower their young leaders to care for the spiritual destinies of their friends as much as prom dates, football games, grades, college preparation, and other extra-curricular activities. The goal here is not to establish Christendom or engage in debates about how closely America's past or present reflects a Christian nation. Instead, the point is that the majority of our nation's young people gather in schools with no chance of experiencing the transforming love of Jesus or participating in the life of God's kingdom unless business as usual changes for many youth pastors and churches. For the sake of young people who God desperately longs for a relationship with, the church must seize the day and engage the one place where youth spend the majority of their time, energy, and social capital: America's public schools.

As mentioned earlier, we do not know how long the legal window will remain open that allows us to stand alongside student leaders as invited guests on their campuses. Let's make the most of every opportunity.[105] Our nation's public schools are filled with young people longing for love, hope, purpose, and direction. They yearn for a family to belong to, a cause to believe in, and a dream to inspire them. At their core – whether they realize it or not – they are longing for Jesus. He is the only good shepherd capable of satisfying a human soul. As God's people who experience his calming presence leading us beside still waters, can we dare keep the waters of life to ourselves? When the coming generation attempts to quench their thirst for life through generic spirituality but does not know the one true God, can we allow them to wander in the desolate desert while we remain refreshed with our thirst quenched? The great thing about living water is that it can never run dry.[106] We may run out of time at the end of a day or money at the end of a month. But the life, forgiveness, power, presence, fellowship, and purpose of Christ can never run out, no matter how many times we give it away. The world is dying of thirst and we have an unlimited supply of living water to share.

When we withdraw into a protective life inside a bubble, we often do so out of a sincere desire to guard our children and loved ones from the corrosive forces around us. In theory, life in the bubble sounds like a great concept. But counterintuitively, it can also lead to death – not just for those on the outside who lack living water – but those on inside can be at risk too.

Scientists at the the University of Arizona designed a "biosphere" project meant to replicate all the ideal conditions for life on Earth inside of an artificial dome. With great motives, they built a large transparent sphere and layered the floor with nutrient-rich soil. All the plants and trees enjoyed the perfect amount of sunlight. They regulated the temperature to optimize growing conditions. Water and fertilizer were plentiful. Weeds and dangerous bugs got eliminated. Everything growing under the dome had ample room to expand inside the giant transparent "bubble."

Scientists thought they had carefully orchestrated a plant utopia where all things green could flourish and thrive. To their amazement, however, nearly every tree and plant in the biosphere experiment died. It was not for lack of sunlight, water, optimal air quality, good soil, fertilizer, spacing, protection, or care. Instead, researchers discovered that the trees lacked an unexpected yet critical ingredient to their long-term health: wind! Without wind pushing hard against the trees and plants, their roots would not be forced deeper into the soil. Wind "teaches" a tree to stand its ground and allows it to forge a solid and lasting foundation. Protecting the trees from all resistance ended up costing them their lives. In the spiritual realm, deep roots only come through opposition which forces us to define what we are going to stand for and what our lives are built on. Without resistance to our faith, we do not establish a root system strong enough to endure all of life's challenges.

My genuine fear for many children raised exclusively in private Christian schools and home school environments is that they can inadvertently end up living in a "biosphere" that does not provide enough wind (exposure to competing ideas, contrasts, opposition, resistance) blowing against their faith-based worldview to drive roots deep into the soil. With wonderful intentions, parents seek to protect young people from harmful elements of our culture but end up isolating them in ways that prevent deep growth and engagement. Self-discovery, relationships with those who are different, and the exploration of competing ideas allow young people to formulate their own identity in Christ when guided by the truth of scripture. This process requires them to back their bag of beliefs for themselves instead of simply carrying their parent's inherited belief system around with them.[107] Engaging others in public schools provides students with the opportunity to put their own roots down while also being salt and light to friends who need what they have. According to one parable of Jesus, the hard rains will indeed come, strong winds are guaranteed to blow, but Christ promises that the house built on the rock (obeying the word of God) will stand through the storm.[108]

I dream of a day when congregations, pastors, and youth pastors view their "parish" as the entire community instead of the four walls of a church building or a private educational institution alone. What if the well-being of the surrounding neighborhood became the measuring stick of success for a local church instead of the inside attendance or budget? I have a strong suspicion that seeking God's kingdom first by pursuing the former will have a positive impact upon the latter too. As Jesus instructs his followers, "Seek ye first the kingdom of God and his righteousness (read: *right relationships*), and all these things will be added unto you as well."[109]

Here at UYC, we offer coaching, training, workshops, resources, guest preachers, and speakers to equip your congregation or organization to engage in effective and holistic campus ministry. If your church would like to take the courageous step into campus ministry, we would love to hear from you so we can walk together.

Feel free to stay in touch with us through Urban Youth Collaborative's website (www.uyc.org). We welcome donations, stories, questions, and opportunities to partner together. My preaching website is also a good way to stay connected (www.natelandis.org) and book a sermon, talk, or training session related to any of this material. Since we truly are called to be a "collaborative" movement, we have also included the contact information of other organizations we trust who are active in campus ministry. They can also help guide and connect you along the way. We are not concerned that you work with us specifically, although we would love that! We just want to see God's people join Jesus in going after a lost generation.

Urban Youth Collaborative
P.O. Box 124708
San Diego, CA 92112
www.uyc.org || www.natelandis.org

nine

CONTACTS AND NEXT STEPS

G et connected and stay connected! Do not feel the pressure to go it alone. Partnering together allows you to benefit from the experience, insights, resources, and relationships of those who have gone before you. They are already in the game. UYC is available for training, coaching, mentoring, ministry development, and project design within America and Mexico's campus ministry space. We would love to learn to know you! Any of the campus ministry partners listed below would love to connect with you too. May God bless you on the adventure of following Jesus to public schools in meaningful and eternal ways!

Urban Youth Collaborative
P.O. Box 124708
San Diego, CA 92112
www.uyc.org
www.natelandis.org

Concrete and Canvas
P.O. Box 2129
National City, CA 91951
www.concreteandcanvas.org

Campus Alliance
P.O. Box 28342
San Diego, CA 92190
www.everyschool.com

Dare to Share
www.dare2share.org

Fellowship of Christian Athletes
8701 Leeds Road
Kansas City, MO 64129
www.fca.org

First Priority
5120 North Federal Highway
Fort Lauderdale, FL 33308
www.firstpriority.cc

Gabe Salazar
www.gabesalazar.com

The Great Opportunity
(Sponsored by Pinetops Foundation)
www. GreatOpportunity.org

Gridiron Ministries
www.gridironministries.com

iThink Big School Assemblies
www.ithinkbig.org

National Network of Youth Ministries
P.O. Box 501748
San Diego, CA 92150
www.nnym.org

National School Project
16175 Whittier Boulevard
Whittier, CA 90603
www.nationalschoolproject.com

Rescue A Generation
P.O. Box 640
Patton, CA 92369-0640
www.rescueageneration.org

Thrive Collective
Office / Studio
132 West 14th Street, 5th Floor
New York, NY 10011
www.thrivecollective.org

Urban Youth Workers Institute
www.uywi.org

Young Life
www.younglife.org

APPENDIX

Re: Legal Guidelines Regarding Faith-Based Clubs on Public Secondary School Campuses

Dear School Official:

The National Center for Law & Policy (NCLP) specializes in First Amendment civil rights issues, including the freedom of speech and the free exercise of religion. We have successfully handled many cases involving the constitutional right of students to form faith-based clubs on public secondary school campuses.

If you are reading this letter, you are probably interacting with a student or an adult non-school volunteer regarding the exercise of well-established constitutional rights. The purpose of this letter is to explain the nature and scope of the legal protections afforded to all citizens, including our clients. In summary, pursuant to the First Amendment and the Equal Access Act (EAA) students must be allowed by state officials to form student-initiated and student-led faith-based clubs on public secondary school campuses, free from any form of government targeting, intolerance, or discrimination, subject to very limited exceptions. Below, you will find the legal guidelines that you should be aware of and must comply with as a public servant, in bullet point form.

LEGAL GUIDELINES FOR FAITH-BASED CLUBS

- Faith-based clubs (FBC) must be allowed to form and meet at public schools and must be treated equally by the school and ASB in all respects as are all other non-curriculum related clubs. In addition to the religious content of FBCs, schools cannot discriminate against the political, philosophical, or other contents of the speech at such meetings.

- FBC's are legally protected, quite robustly so, by the U.S. Constitution's First Amendment (freedom of speech and free exercise of religion) and the federal Equal Access Act (EAA).110

- "Equal access" for FBCs includes, but is not limited to, access to school facilities, resources, websites, announcements, newsletters, bulletin boards, year books, promotional opportunities, facilities, etc., on the same or equal terms as other non-curriculum related clubs.

- FBCs must be student-initiated and student led; student attendance and participation must be voluntary.

- FBC activities may include a wide variety of secular and religious activities including announcements, inviting guest speakers, games, food, Bible study (or discussion of other religious books), prayer, etc.

- FBC meetings and the religious content of FBC activities may not be directed or controlled by school administrators, faculty, or staff, but rather the student leaders.

- FBC activities must not be restricted by the school in any way, unless the meetings materially and substantially interfere with the orderly conduct of educational activities within the school.

- FBCs may have a faculty sponsor, but the sponsor, as a state employee, may not lead the FBC, participate, or otherwise promote religion.

- FBC student leaders, as an extension of their First Amendment rights, may invite outside speakers or guests to speak at or participate in meetings and may receive support, financial assistance, and/or encouragement from, but not be under the control or direct influence of a community organization.

- Guests and speakers invited by the students are permitted to participate in FBC activities, promote religion, and invite students at the meetings to off-campus activities and events. However, non-school persons may not direct, conduct, control, or regularly attend FBC's.

- The Establishment Clause, the so-called separation of church and state, may not be used as an excuse by the school to deny the recognition of a FBC, treat FBCs differently from other clubs, or be misapplied to discriminate against FBC leaders or members as second-class citizens. State employees are only individuals who can violate the Establishment Clause on public school campuses, not students or their invited guests.

- School officials may not allow legally-confused, complaining faculty, students, or community members to exercise a "heckler's veto" against lawful FBCs, improperly asserting that FBCs are not allowed because of a misunderstanding of the "separation of church and state."

Thank you for your anticipated cooperation and respect for students' civil rights. If you have any questions, please feel free to contact me personally at the National Center for Law & Policy or on my office phone at (760) 747-4529.

Sincerely,

Dean R. Broyles, Esq. President & Chief Counsel
THE NATIONAL CENTER FOR LAW & POLICY

UYC's STATEMENT OF FAITH:

1. The Bible
We believe the sixty-six canonical books of the Bible as originally written were inspired of God and therefore free from error. They constitute the only infallible guide in faith and practice.

2. The Triune God
We believe there is one God, creator and sustainer of all things, infinite in being and perfection. He exists eternally in three Persons; the Father, the Son, and the Holy Spirit, who are of one substance and equal in power and glory.

3. Humanity and Sin
We believe humans are created in the image of God and therefore possess intrinsic and eternal value. Through disobedience, God's beloved children fell from their sinless state and plunged into a state of separation from God, estrangement from neighbor, and spiritual death. This also brought upon the entire race the sentence of eternal death. Humans can only be saved from this condition by the grace of God, through faith in the work of Jesus Christ alone.

4. Jesus Christ
We believe in the eternally pre-existent Son who became incarnate without human father, born of the virgin Mary. In the Lord Jesus Christ, the divine and human natures united in one Person, both natures being whole, perfect, and distinct. To make salvation

possible, Jesus lived a sinless life and died on the cross as the sinner's substitute, shedding His blood for the remission of sins. Christ's sacrifice was sufficient to cover the sins of all who repent, and this salvation shall be preached to all people. On the third day, He rose from the dead in the body which has been laid in the tomb. He ascended to the right hand of the Father, where He performs the ministry of intercession. He shall come again, personally and visibly to complete His saving work and to consummate the eternal plan of God.

5. The Holy Spirit

We believe that the Holy Spirit is the third Person of the Triune God. He empowers the church and convicts the world of sin. He applies the work of Christ to humans who believe. Through repentance, justification, and adoption, humans receive a right standing before God. By regeneration and sanctification, a believer's nature becomes renewed.

6. Salvation and Mission

We believe that Christian disciples, having turned to God in penitent faith in the Lord Jesus Christ are accountable to God for living a life separated from sin, marked by obedience to Scriptural commandments, and characterized by the fruit of the Spirit. It is their responsibility to contribute by word and deed to the universal spread of the Gospel and the advancement of the kingdom of God.

7. The End of the Age

At the end of the age, we believe the bodies of the dead shall be raised. The righteous shall enter into full possession of eternal life in God's presence. The wicked shall be condemned to eternal punishment apart from God and His goodness.

8. Sacraments

We believe that the Sacraments were instituted by God through the ministry of Jesus. They seal us in our redemption, confirm our identity as members of God's covenant community, and mark us to participate in the church's mission. In Baptism, we participate in Jesus' death and resurrection; it is the sign and seal of oneness with Him. It symbolizes the washing and cleansing of sin through Christ. In the Lord's Supper we eat and drink in communion with the crucified and risen Lord. This unites us with Christ and fellow believers who gather around the table in the presence of our Lord.

ENDNOTES

1 This was the figure given to me by the nurse at the Escondido, California hospital where my son was born.

2 www.the-hospitalist.org/hospitalist/article/123116/code-pink (accessed on September 21, 2017).

3 www.ecology.com/birth-death-rates/ (accessed on September 21, 2017).

4 This statistic comes from an informal survey we conducted when UYC began in 2008 where we compared youth group attendance to middle and high school populations in San Diego Unified School District.

5 John 10:10

6 Matthew 7:21-23

7 Matthew 28:16-20

8 I am a strong advocate for the importance of responsible global missions. According to the model spelled out in Acts 1:8, we should begin in Jerusalem (city), spread out through Judea (county), Samaria (state), and finally head to the ends of the earth (world). My goal is to make sure Christians do not ignore the "mission field" right beside them: local public schools across the street.

9 Depending on how one interprets Barna's definition of a true believer, the statistics of decline vary somewhat. Nonetheless, a clear trend away from belief in foundational Christian beliefs and behaviors remains.

10 John 1:14a

11 Matthew 4:19 (NASB)

12 I read this in an article from the National Network of Youth Ministries magazine years ago (date elusive) and it has stuck with me ever since.

13 Ibid.

14 John 1:29

15 Duffy Robbins mentored me during my four years as a youth ministry student at Eastern University. He is on the short list of greatest influences in my life.

16 The forum and content of a motivational school assembly differs from that of a student-led faith club. The former is non-religious while the later can be specifically Christian in content. We partner with iThink Big School Assemblies for these presentations because they excel at communicating an inspiring and worthwhile message to audiences in a public school context.

17 John Leland, "Savior of the Streets." *Newsweek*. June 1, 1998.

18 Saint Augustine. *Confessions*, Translated by F.J. Sheed, (New York, Sheed & Ward, 1942).

19 This plaque now appears below the statue of Jesus in front of Christ the King Catholic Church in San Diego. I heard the story about the vandalism incidents and subsequent business meeting described by Pastor Shawn Mitchell at a Luis Palau CityFest event held in San Diego in 2010.

20 Harold Camping reportedly accepted donations from people who sold their homes and liquidated long-term life savings accounts to finance his specifically-timed, end-of-the-world message. www.washingtonpost.com/local/obituaries/harold-camping-radio-evangelist-who-predicted-doomsday-dies-at-92/2012/05/16/gJQAlgpxAp_story.html?utm_term=.feeb68796114 (accessed on June 8, 2018).

21 The 1990s hip-hop artist "Coolio" coined this phrase to describe the challenges present in the communities he grew up in. This song came out when I first began the adventure of cross-cultural ministry in an urban setting. I listened to it while driving through Philadelphia and contemplating the stories of the young people I was learning to know and care for.

22 www.sandiegouniontribune.com/news/public-safety/sd-me-fatal-shooting-valencia-20180121-story.html (accessed on September 10, 2018).

23 This is the tagline of the new *Exorcist* TV series.

24 Matthew 16:18

25 In John 10:10, Jesus says that the thief comes only to steal, kill, and destroy. But he has come to bring life to the fullest.

26 Exodus 4:10

27 Exodus 4:2

28 Genesis 46:34

29 Romans 12:18

30 2 Timothy 3:12

31 I even got concerned calls from principals at two private high schools in San Diego that were unaffiliated with San Diego Unified School District. The professional lobbyist attacking us was so upset that she made sure to "warn" these other schools about us too.

32 Such an announcement is not required by law. This particular student club chose to begin their meeting that way on the day of the parent complaint.

33 www.voiceofsandiego.org/topics/education/documents-raise-major-questions-about-school-districts-quality-assurance-office/ (accessed on October 23, 2017)

34 www.law.cornell.edu/uscode/text/20/4071 (accessed on May 31, 2018)

35 Ibid.

36 Dean Broyles told me that, when serving in religious liberties cases, he is a "sledgehammer for the Lord." As a pacifist from a Mennonite background, I was not sure how to take this.

37 www.sandiegounified.org/addressing-bullying-muslim-students (accessed on September 10, 2018).

38 I am deeply grateful for the hundreds of hours of free legal work provided attorney Dean Broyles and the National Center for Law & Policy to Urban Youth Collaborative and the student club leaders. This saved our ministry and the students approximately $80,000 to $100,00 dollars.

39 Ephesians 5:16

40 1 Timothy 4:12

41 John 11:25

42 I head Greg Stier share this insight at one of his Dare to Share youth ministry training events in San Diego in 2015.

43 James 5:16b

44 James 3:4-5

45 This phrase comes from Dr. Kent Edwards, one of my preaching professors at Gordon-Conwell Theological Seminary.

46 I got this line from Tony Campolo, my professor at Eastern University, who used it to humorously describe the way God makes certain things so obvious to us that it cannot be ignored.

47 Matthew 18:3-4

48 Luke 18:16

49 My friend Mark Bell served as the youth pastor at The Rock Church when we first dreamed about Project 25 together.

50 Genesis 50:20 (NLT)

51 This powerful charge came to me from my dear brother, Pastor Adrian Ewings. It has become such a key part of my ministry that I often end sermons with this story to this day.

52 John 17:16

53 The Center for Urban Ministerial Education (CUME) at GCTS did emphasize the importance of holistic ministry within the context of complex city environments.

54 Charles Finney, *The Original Memoirs of Charles Finney*, (Grand Rapids: Zondervan Publishing House, 2002), 272.

55 Kyla Calvert, "Graduation Rates Inch Up Across State, San Diego County," KPBS, April 9, 2013, www.kpbs.org/news/2013/apr/09/graduation-rates-inch-across-state-sd-county/ (accessed on February 15, 2015).

56 Ibid.

57 Jonathan Kozol, *Savage Inequalities: Children in America's Schools*, (New York, Harper Perennial, 1992), 2.

58 Luke 10:2

59 "The whole gospel for the whole world" comes from Eastern University's useful motto during my undergraduate years.

60 Pastor Harvey Carey shared this insight during a plenary address at the Urban Youth Workers Institute on May 16, 2008.

61 Hebrews 10:25

62 John 15:13

63 Luke 5:6-10a

64 Luke 5:6

65 Luke 5:7

66 John 5:8

67 C.S. Lewis, *The Weight of Glory: And Other Addresses*, (New York, Harper-Collins Publishers, 1980).

68 Luke 5:10

69 John 21:9-11

70 Saint Jerome, Translated and introduced by Thomas P. Scheck, *Commentary on Ezekiel*, (New York, Newman Press, 2017), 569.

71 John would not have been aware of the later sources Saint Jerome cites. Yet the possibility remains that many representative species of fish could have been miraculously caught in the net with Jesus' help. Having every existing Mediterranean species of fish present would not be required to make a significant theological and prophetic point about the diverse and universal composition of the future church.

72 H. Garcia, "Odd Numbers and their Theological Potential," *Mathematics and the Divine: A Historical Study*, ed. Teun Koetsier and Luc Bergmans, (New York, Elsevier, 2005), pp. 241.

73 On display in Bethel Seminary of San Diego.

74 This concept of the "homogeneous unity principle" is advocated by church growth strategist Peter Wagner in *Our Kind of People: The Ethical Dimensions of Church Growth in America* and *Your Church Can Grow: Seven Vital Signs of a Healthy Church*.

75 Acts 2:5

76 Acts 2:9-11, 41

77 C.S. Lewis, *The Screwtape Letters*, (originally 1942; this edition: Harper Collins, 1996), ix.

78 Dr. Ray Bakke shared this insight during a plenary address at the Urban Youth Workers Institute (UYWI) Conference in May of 2006.

79 Matthew 6:33

80 Professor Michael Mata shared this insight in his course "Urban Context of Theology and Ministry" at Claremont School of Theology during the spring of 2008.

81 Matthew 6:10

82 James 4:7

83 I first heard this vivid phrase used by Michael Brunker who serves as Executive Director of the Jackie Robinson YMCA in San Diego.

84 Robert Wuthnow, *The Restructuring of American Religion: Society and Faith Since World War II*, (Princeton, Princeton University Press, 1990), 254.

85 This comment came during the public question and answer time that followed his address. The full transcript is available by viewing Western Michigan University's archives at: wmich.edu/sites/default/files/attachments/MLK.pdf (accessed on January 20, 2015).

86 Professor Vincent Wimbush shared this observation during a course on scriptures and race at Claremont Graduate University in the fall of 2006.

87 www.sandiegouniontribune.com/news/education/sd-me-hoover-high-20170812-story.html (accessed on September 25, 2017).

88 Professor Michael Mata shared this insight during a course on urban ecclesiology at Claremont School of Theology in the spring of 2008.

89 When discussing "theological partisanship," I am referring to non-essential tenants that believes allow to become more important than the shared essential core doctrines that unite all believers in Christ.

90 *"In necessariis unitas, in dubiis libertas, in omnibus caritas,"* or "in necessary things unity; in uncertain things liberty; in all things charity," attributed to Archbishop of Split (Spalato) Marco Antonio de Dominis, 1617. ("book 4, chapter 8," *De republica ecclesiastica libri X*, 1, (London), p. 676.)

91 The righteousness – or lack thereof – of our horizontal relationships with others, similarly and simultaneously, has a direct impact on our vertical relationship with God.

92 Proverbs 29:18 (KJV)

93 Luke 15

94 www.pewtrusts.org/en/research-and-analysis/blogs/stateline/2013/11/15/ states-insist-on-third-grade-reading-proficiency (accessed on November 1, 2017).

95 www.begintoread.com/research/literacystatistics.html (accessed on November 1, 2017)

96 www.pewtrusts.org/en/research-and-analysis/blogs/stateline/2013/11/15/ states-insist-on-third-grade-reading-proficiency (accessed on November 1, 2017).

97 1 Corinthians 9:19-23

98 I picked these three-fold levels of community engagement up from Pastor Sam Williams at Gateway Church in El Cajon, California.

99 Mother Teresa of Calcutta and the Missionaries of Charity, *Works of Love Are Works of Peace*, A Photographic Record by Michael Collopy, (San Francisco, Ignatius Press, 1996), 105.

100 *Good News Club v. Milford Central School*, 533 U.S. 98 (2001)

101 Fuller Youth Institute's "Sticky Faith" initiative has documented that between 63-94% of high school students from mainline denominations walk away from their faith during their college years.

102 The Barna Group claims that as many as 94% of Christians make a decision to follow Jesus by age 18.

103 record.adventistchurch.com/2017/05/19/george-barna-tells-adventist-delegates-we-are-in-a-crisis/ (accessed on September 25, 2017).

104 Ibid.

105 Ephesians 5:16

106 John 7:38

107 Here again I thank my mentor, Duffy Robbins, for this helpful image and insight.

108 Matthew 7:24-27

109 Matthew 6:33

110 20 U.S.C. §4071 ("It shall be unlawful for any public secondary school which receives Federal financial assistance and which has a limited open forum to deny equal access or a fair opportunity to, or discriminate against, any students who wish to conduct a meeting within that limited open forum on the basis of religion, political, philosophical or other content of the speech at such meetings." (emphasis added); See also, Westside Community Board of Education v. Mergens, 496 U.S. 226 (1990).